Mother's WORK

Pearls of Wisdom & Gems from my journey

Carol T. Muleta

Copyright © 2021 Return On Intelligence, LLC

Copyright © 2021 Return On Intelligence, LLC

All rights reserved. No part of this book may be reproduced or transmitted in any form or by any means, electronic, or mechanical, including photocopying, recording or by any information storage and retrieval system, without permission from the author, except for the inclusion of brief quotations in a review.

Printed in the United States of America

Muleta, Carol T.

Mother's Work: Pearls of Wisdom & Gems from my journey

ISBN: 978-1-7352635-3-3

Warning - Disclaimer

The purpose of this book is to inform and entertain. The author and publisher shall have neither liability nor responsibility to any person or entity with respect to any loss or damage caused, or alleged to have been caused, directly or indirectly, by the information contained in this book.

It is not the purpose of this book to provide an exhaustive reference or guide on all aspects of parenting, childcare, and family life. You are urged to read all available information, learn as much as possible about parenting, and tailor the information to your individual needs.

Parenting is not an exact science. The context and insights offered in this book represent an account of the author's experience for the reader's information and consideration. The author and the publisher decline to guarantee any specific parenting outcomes for anyone reading this book and/or taking actions described herein.

Every effort has been made to make this work as complete and accurate as possible. However, there may be mistakes, both typographical, and in content. Therefore, this text should be used only as a general guide and not as the ultimate source for parent education or advice. The author has tried to recreate events, locales, and conversations from her memories of them. In order to maintain their anonymity, in some instances the author has changed the names of individuals and places and may have changed some identifying characteristics and details such as physical properties, occupations and places of residence.

For My Tribe - John, Matt, and Zach

This journey would not have been possible without you. Thank you for crawling, walking, skipping, and running it with me. It has been an unforgettable adventure.

Mother's Work: Pearls of Wisdom & Gems from my journey

Preface i
Acknowledgements ix
Introduction xvii
How to Use this Book........................... xxiii
Chapter 1: Purpose 1
Chapter 2: Faith 13
Chapter 3: Courage 29
Chapter 4: Wisdom 57
Chapter 5: Love & Friendship 69
Chapter 6: Presence 95
Chapter 7: Peace 105
A FINAL WORD 113
Appendix A 115
   Real Beauty 115
About the Author 119
About The Parenting 411® 121

Mother's Work

Mother's Work

Preface

For some, motherhood (or parenthood) is another marker or milestone in the course of adulting – think graduation from high school and college, career advancement, marriage, etc. I will admit becoming a mother was an aspiration for me. It felt like something I *should* want to do. The man I married certainly wanted children, so we set out to try and make it happen.

It wasn't long before I realized becoming a parent is a completely different kind of milestone. I certainly give honor to God for everything I have even been able to accomplish. With other endeavors like succeeding in school, earning degrees, and realizing career success, I could at least have the illusion that it was all due to my hard work and nothing else, if I were so inclined. But this baby-making thing? That happens in God's time. As we pursued parenthood, I marveled anew at the miracle conception truly is. There is a divine alignment of several earthly elements that has to occur within a narrow window of time, or the opportunity is gone; until the next month, or the next month and so on. That God is able to bring forth life through the lowly vessels that are our physical bodies is a profound miracle; not a marker and no mere milestone. Caring for the fruit of that

Mother's Work

effort would not be an accomplishment or reward, but my ministry. This was the first of many lessons about motherhood. These lessons became pearls of wisdom that I clutched tightly as I steered my way through the trials, triumphs, and "too funny for words" moments of being a mom.

Before I became "Mom," I was just me. I was the youngest of three children and grew up in Washington, DC. I was a little on the quiet side, but I had lot of energy and spent a good deal of time outside, playing with friends. I'm fairly easy-going and chill today, but back then I was always on the move and up for any physical challenge. I always did rather well in school, so my mother indulged my interests. I ventured into ballet, gymnastics, cheerleading, Girl Scouts, track & field, modeling, and volleyball. Despite being the child of tall parents and growing to be 6 feet tall, I wouldn't learn to play basketball until I fell in love with the game while watching my own sons play.

Heading into high school, I had planned to study to be an optometrist. Inexplicably, in my junior year, I decided I wanted to go into the fashion industry. After graduation from college with a degree in fashion merchandising, I did work in the industry for about two years. To my surprise, I didn't love it, so I transitioned to the federal government, where I applied my talents in forecasting, planning, and

Mother's Work

analysis to a new gig -- managing a multimillion-dollar inventory program for naval aviation electronics. Of course, I looked stylish doing it.

After about three years, I set off again. This time, I went to graduate school. Two years later, I emerged with an MBA degree and a budding romance with my future husband. All of the hard work and sacrifice had paid off -- handsomely, even. And, importantly, I felt equipped to pursue the career in marketing I desired.

I was, in fact, equipped to do many things, though I didn't fully appreciate it then. I landed at a quasi-government agency and hung out there much longer this time – 10 years! By the time I left, I had become a Senior Marketing Program Manager, where I managed a product portfolio exceeding $1 billion in annual revenue. I enjoyed the people I worked with and we had a mutual respect that allowed us to accomplish great things together. However, that role ended because my life was about to *change*.

I left my office on a Friday afternoon, fully expecting to return to work Monday, lead a workshop series, finish out the week, and THEN take a well-deserved rest for two weeks as I prepared to give birth to our wonder twins. This was MY plan, but they had *other* plans – they showed up early, and I never made it back to the office to do the workshop or anything else.

Mother's Work

I even missed the surprise baby shower my colleagues had planned! The sacrifice has been well worth it, though I AM hoping to recoup that two-week vacation one of these days. Anyway, I became a happy mom, a tired mom; a sometimes exhausted and delirious mom (hey, sleep deprivation is REAL!).

I should tell you that in my adventures up to this point, there was one thing I *never* envisioned doing – becoming a stay-at-home mother. It was not part of my detailed life plan, and friends and family can tell you that I declared, emphatically, it would not *ever* be part of my plan. I certainly hoped to get married one day and have children. I just didn't think I would sacrifice my career growth and give my undivided attention to those endeavors. It is a perfectly respectable choice, but it simply wasn't what I saw growing up in my family and among the families of my friends. Most of our mothers were educated, like our fathers, and they worked outside of the home, like our fathers. Having said ALL of that, I don't believe I would be here doing this work that fulfills me in a way that NO other job ever has, had I not done this thing I said I would NEVER do.

After those early months at home with my dynamic duo, I became restless, thinking about my next move. I decided to launch a marketing and sales consulting company. This was a difficult undertaking that first year and my little guys weren't exactly going with the

Mother's Work

flow. I mean, why should they? They had plans too. They were a bit of a handful (or two hands full), and I made the choice to set aside my ambitions for a moment and focus on my boys.

While I tended to their needs and explored the world with them, I spent time reading and taking classes to learn as much as I could about children and how they develop. I even became a certified parent educator with a highly regarded, non-profit organization and began to co-lead parenting classes, and for four years, served on the organization's Board of Directors. Since the beginning of my experience there, I have been sharing what I learned, first informally among friends. Later, I combined these learnings with my own perspectives and other experiences, and all this informed my subsequent work with community organizations I served.

As I ended my term as president of one of these groups, a support group for mothers of color, I settled down for a good night's sleep after a somewhat stressful year in office and in life. I almost immediately received a message from God in a dream and He let me know *change* was coming. The message went something like this, "I want you to start a company and share what you know." I was highly skeptical -- "God, nobody wants to hear me speak." He said, "Not only will they listen to you, they will also **pay** to hear you speak." This was becoming a full-blown dialogue now. "God, how will I do that when I don't know how to …," I asked. For every obstacle I identified, he named a specific person(s) in my life who could help me overcome it. Still, unconvinced, I responded, "You know [insert name] is busy, she won't be able to help me." (Don't ask me why, but He only mentioned women.) He, in turn, responded by encouraging me to overcome my reluctance and seek their assistance. He also made it clear I was to make a plan but wait until the boys entered kindergarten to execute it. When He **stopped** talking, I said, "Wait! You laid this at my feet, and you're done talking? Really, God??? I have so many more questions!!!!"

I'd love to tell you I jumped right in to preparing for this assignment the very next day, but in truth, it took about 5 more years; essentially 3 years longer than when He told me to start. Even then, I only took the first crucial step after an opportunity that I almost overlooked presented itself and I co-founded Gardener Parenting Consultants with another mom.

That was 12 years ago, and it has been a fulfilling experience for me to work with parents and families. Today, I create and present parenting classes and webinars, and provide consultation for parents. I also guide parents in developing the unique tools and resources they need to support their children's healthy growth and development, instill confidence and self-discipline, and promote harmony in the family.

It has been my privilege to meet many like-minded professionals who also serve families, and to collaborate with them on special projects outside of the company. It was one such meeting that led me to step out on faith again and launch a radio show, Parenting 411 – yet another *change,* although I'd been preparing for it for years without even realizing it. In January 2015, I joined Team Radio Baltimore, a team of dynamic, accomplished women with expertise in various areas offering a full array of programming on WOLB 1010 AM Talk Radio. My show is Parenting 411, where we provide "information parents need from sources they can trust."

That is how I got here. It's been a great ride and it's not over! I'm still a mom, just not as hands-on, now that my sons are young adults. I'm loving this phase of my life and I wanted to share what I've learned with you. I hope it will resonate with you and give you some reassurance that you are more than up to the job. Along the way, you learn so much about your children and even more about yourself. Stay alert -- there's always something new around the corner. If you're open to trying something new, almost every day (!), this is indeed the gig for you

Mother's Work

Acknowledgments

John Thank you, dear husband, for being my partner on this wild ride. We have navigated a lot of landscape together and I appreciate your patience, enthusiasm, and encouragement. Along with your unwavering love, they have been a capacious well of strength and security for me.

Matt My first-born (by a minute), I am awed by you. You have always been resolute about acting with purpose and not merely for others' entertainment or approval. Your work ethic and discipline have helped you scale mountains that others thought were too high. You are highly empathetic, and your kindness and compassion for others are almost too good for this world, sometimes. We are profoundly thankful, nonetheless.

Zach Your courage and energy have made you a true force from the beginning. When you make up your mind about something, you don't stop until you get it. Keep that energy as you pursue the goals you have carefully mapped out. I have always been fascinated with how you are able to wake up each morning with a fresh outlook, regardless of what happened the day before. Your curiosity as a boy was sometimes challenging, but invariably entertaining. Keep that sparkle in your eyes, son!

My dear mother, Meta Williams As I reflect on my own motherhood journey, I realize how much I owe to you. You always gave the best of what you had for your three children, be it time, talent, encouragement. You even gave your last dollar when you thought it was going to make a difference in our lives. Growing up, I always thought you had very high standards and expected me to be perfect. I realize now that you were just teaching me to function in the world and to rise to any occasion with confidence and grace. I know I haven't been perfect, but I have always tried to stay connected to God and be kind to others because you modeled that for me. I was asked once to name a fondest memory of my Mom and there are too many memories that I cherish to narrow it down to just one. However, there is one from recent years that truly captures your nature. I came over one afternoon after teaching a class and spent the rest of the day with you. I was so sleepy, and you told me to go up to "my room" and take a nap. After I got under the covers, you tiptoed in and laid a blanket on me, just right. That was the sweetest sleep ever! You extended that love and care to my sons and were very playful with them when they were young. I joked once that if you had been that fun when I was growing up, I would have had the coolest mom on the block. To that you responded, "You *did* have the coolest mom on the block." I feel proud and blessed to be your child and pray that my children can say the same of me.

My father, Jefferson Melvin Thank you for the model for creating a vision and diligently pursuing it, no matter what, or who, gets in the way. With perseverance and tenacity you pursued an education through the GI bill, gaining the admiration of your college classmates we would learn years later. I have come to appreciate how your personal journey shaped your tough love and emphasis on instilling self-discipline and a strong work ethic in us.

Brother Terrence Thank you for watching over me growing up. You were my first spiritual guide and I greatly admire your courage and commitment to your faith. You are a solid man of God and walk out His purpose in your life everywhere – family, ministry, and your profession.

Sister Gwen You are a model mom. I admire the family you have created. The fierce love, loyalty, and affection you all have is beautiful to witness. Thank you for being the voice of reason and wisdom we can turn to when we need direction.

Stepfather Zack I like to say you were a gentleman among men. I felt pretty grown-up when you married Mom and joined our family. I was happy for the prospect of her spending her golden years with you and that was good enough for me. Yet, I still learned so much from you. Your life story, from your pilgrimage from home in Texas at a young age and your valiant service to our country in three branches of the military to your entrepreneurial pursuits, you had a dogged determination to make it and to bless your family with the fruits of your labors. My fondness and love for you are rooted in your courage, resourcefulness, and your kindness. You lived a model life.

My in-laws, The Muleta Family You have been very much a part of my journey to this point. You have showered love and adoration on our family as grandparents, aunts, and uncles and a legion of cousins I adore immensely. We have shared so many good times filled with food, fun, and fellowship. Thank you, thank you.

My first friends, Michelle Davis and Angelia Bland Anyone who knows me knows I have a host of girlfriends. And I have treasured them all. At risk of leaving someone out, I won't try to name everyone, though I do want to acknowledge my first friends. After my brother, Michelle was probably my first-ever playmate as a toddler. We've had some adventures and amusements I will never forget. When they saw you coming, my family braced themselves for what you and I might get ourselves into next. I must also acknowledge the warmth and acceptance your family showed me as I was growing up as your friend -- I went a lot of places with y'all! Angelia and I became fast friends in first grade. We, too, have had our fair share of madcap schemes, mischief, and mayhem. And we survived! We continued our academic journey together through high school before venturing off on our own for college. Your courage and common sense have not only served you well, but have also been a blessing to me, too. Ladies, thank you both so much for your support and encouragement through the years, including serving as godmothers to my wonder twins. I pray that I have been able to return the favor.

Alpha Kappa Alpha Sorority, Inc.; Mocha Moms, Inc.; and Jack & Jill of America, Inc. I am so grateful to be a part of these wonderful organizations that have enhanced my journey as a woman and a mom. The first organization I joined on my own, for my own reasons, was the great and first of its kind, Alpha Kappa Alpha Sorority, Inc. I joined a phenomenal sisterhood and learned so much about service and leadership. That foundation propelled me through my career, post-graduate education, and my fellowship with sister-friends across the globe. I am so thankful to my sorority sisters and our advisors for pouring into me as a young woman. My connection with Mocha Moms, Inc. came at another seminal moment as I ventured into motherhood. This support group for moms of color provided a welcome respite and safe space for "real talk" as we all figured out this parenting (and family) thing together. I have marveled at how it has grown into an international force on behalf of mothers of color. Finally, Jack & Jill of America, Inc. welcomed me into another sister-circle of mothers of black children committed to providing enriching experiences for their own offspring, as well as children in their communities. I am so grateful for the support shown to me, personally and professionally, and the love and leadership lavished on my children during our family's involvement in the Northern Virginia Chapter.

Parent Encouragement Program I was already committed to being the best parent I could be, *and* I was in search of some tools and a little guidance. We all know there is no real instruction book for parenting. So, it was here that my curiosity about parenting lovingly and courageously was met with warm, caring instructors who happily shared their wisdom, and directed us all toward useful resources. I owe a debt of gratitude to founder, **Linda Jessup**, not only for her vision and commitment to fulfilling a great need in the community and in society, but also for her personal encouragement of me. It was she who drove home the importance of building courage in my then toddler son, Matt, as he took the early steps toward overcoming his developmental challenges. Up to that point, I was focused only on the mounting list of skills he'd need to master without considering the grit and courage it would take to do it. Over the years, Linda's words harkened back to me as I urged Matt to take to heart the words of NBA great Larry Byrd: "Don't give an inch until the final buzzer sounds."

Sheila Gardner Thank you for being one of the first friends I made in Mocha Moms. It has been wonderful watching our children grow up over the years. We took a big step and launched Gardener Parenting Consultants together, pooling our talents, insights, and experiences. The company has been one of several pathways through which I have been able to share my passion for giving parents tools to guide the healthy growth and development of their children. We blessed many families over the years as we shared the Gardener Parent Method®.

Dr. Linda McGhee Thank you for your advice and support as a trusted friend and your service as a professional collaborator. You are a stellar clinician and I admire your commitment to serve with your knowledge and insights. I wish you continued success in your endeavors.

Patsy Anderson Wow, you came into my life at an interesting and amazing time! I am so thankful for your enthusiastic support of me as a radio host on your team. Your patient instruction and guidance gave me a tremendous boost. You had faith when I wasn't so sure! Thank you again and I am proud of the work we have done together.

American Mothers, Inc. Thank you so much for honoring me as the 2019 District of Columbia Mother of the Year®. I also owe a tremendous debt of gratitude to my Soror and dear friend Barbara Owens for nominating me for this recognition. It was such a privilege to be welcomed into an amazing network of courageous, resilient, and dedicated moms from across the country. They are truly a blessing to their families and communities.

Wilma Simons My patient and encouraging editor. Can't believe we are finally putting this out into the world. Thank you so much for your understanding during the fits and starts. I am sure you are as relieved as I am to get this out the door. I hope you are as proud of it as I am. I promise I'll be a much wiser and more efficient client on the next project.

Mother's Work

Introduction

The day I learned I was carrying twins is memorable… and comical. My husband and I had gone to see my doctor for a sonogram. A few months earlier, I had undergone surgery and, while we knew I was pregnant, the doctor who had performed it was making sure all was well. The doctor told us in a mildly excited way that there were two babies. I said, "Cool!" and my husband said, "Whoa!"

A few weeks later, with another sonogram, we would find out we were having two boys. Now, THAT was shocking to me and I said, "But I don't know what to do with boys." I reasoned that I could easily figure out how to mother a girl since I had been one. By the time we headed back to the car, I predicted that having boys in the house would probably be fun! However, there was no doubt about it -- this would be really new for me. I still wondered if I was actually cut out to be a "boy-mom." In fact, I must confess I did include a girl's name on my list when I went to the hospital to deliver, just in case the technician had made the wrong call. She didn't and I can say today that raising boys has been a blast.

Mother's Work

In the beginning, it was a little hectic. Here I thought I would be like a camp counselor, guiding the youngsters in my charge who would look up to me, hang on my every word, and obediently follow my instructions. After all, I had been a decent team leader at my job. How hard could this be? Like I said, it eventually got to be fun, but in the beginning, I was outmanned and outsmarted.

All along, I found our boys to be fascinating and created with individual purpose and possibility. It became my mission to unleash their potential. Because there were two of them, I also felt committed to treating them as individuals, vs. "the twins" whom we should expect to behave the same way, like the same things and dress the same way -- forever. I owe a debt of gratitude to a few adult twins I know who shared some of the horrors they experienced along those lines. I also had to let go of the notion that the boys would fall into the role of my little campers whom I could coax into doing everything as a unit, lockstep and in formation.

It occurred to me that if I wanted to be an effective mother, I needed some tools. First, I read books about twins and young children in general. I also joined a support group for moms of color, Mocha Moms, Inc. When my sons turned two, I took a course led by a local non-profit, the Parent Encouragement Program, Inc. This class launched me in to the world of formal parent education. I was introduced to positive discipline and the teachings of noted psychologist Alfred Adler. His approach to understanding the motivations behind human behavior intermingled with the stages of human development felt right to me and suited my rational mindset. To my total surprise, it also spoke to my heart on a spiritual level. It occurred to me that parenthood was a not an assignment to be muddled through, but a ministry presented by God that I had best honor. Through all the discussion about misbehavior and meltdowns (for parents and kids!), I saw parallels to my journey with God, and the highlights and the low moments along the way.

A new mindset about parenting as ministry was evolving in me. I began to speak about this to other moms I encountered and got blank stares until one day, I shared it with another mom-friend who got it immediately. Fast forward about 5 years and together, we co-founded our own company with this core principle of parenting as ministry underpinning our philosophy. We began to share our philosophy in workshops at schools, churches, conferences – wherever parents or caregivers were gathered. Since that time, I have seized opportunities to reach parents in new ways. First, through radio and speaking engagements. Whenever I presented or sat for interviews on various parenting topics, I was asked about my personal background and I eagerly shared. Every time, I was told I should share more of it to inspire as well as inform parents. Part of my story was my hunt for the answers I needed, since I could never find books that singularly addressed my experience. I wound up reading several and attending lectures on parenting. Though at the time, I was merely taking steps to meet the needs of my children (as mothers do), observers were pointing out that insights I gained along the way could flatten the learning curve for moms in similar situations. These included transitioning from working mom to stay-at-home mom, raising multiples, and navigating development delays and special education. And launching a business while doing any or all these roles. The latter was the topic of my debut as an author in *2020* with my contribution to an anthology entitled <u>Courageous Enough to Launch: Stories and Strategies of Everyday Women Who Faced Their Fears To Launch & Grow Thriving Businesses</u>. I am thankful to be finally sharing more of my story through books.

In *Mother's Work,* I'm going to share with you the lessons and the blessings I have experienced as Mom. Indeed, I do treasure them like precious pearls.

The pearls I have cited in this book provided inspiration and guidance to me while I traveled the path of motherhood that was charted just for me. They gradually revealed themselves to me in a way very much akin to the process through which pearls are created. When an intruder, such as a grain of sand or other particle, makes its way into the shell of an oyster, mussel or clam, the mollusk responds by releasing a substance called nacre that coats the invader several times over as a defensive strategy to protect its organs and the environment within the shell. This determined effort, which can take three years, yields a beautiful pearl.

By wrestling repeatedly with unexpected and often unwanted circumstances that disrupted the environment within the "shell" of my family, these pearls emerged, and motherhood became a thing of beauty for me. As with all treasured possessions, beauty has to be maintained. I did this by being mindful of my experiences, doing research, and gleaning what I could to apply when new challenges entered my shell.

These pearls, and the lessons leading to their creation, served to anchor me as I chartered unknown territory, gaining enlightenment, confronting truths, and challenging assumptions, with the objective of creating a parenting philosophy that worked for our sons and our family.

Pearls of Wisdom

- Purpose
- Faith
- Courage
- Wisdom
- Love & Friendship
- Presence
- Peace

On its face, this collection of pearls seems simple. The underlying lessons are what give it meaning to me. In presenting these pearls, my hope is to encourage and inform other moms. More importantly, it is my sincere wish that you will be inspired to embrace your experiences, whether challenging or exhilarating, to find richer insight that imprints your life and, in turn, takes root in the hearts of your children.

How to Use this Book

Each chapter of the book is devoted to a pearl of wisdom. I share lessons learned, sometimes illustrated in true stories. At the conclusion of each chapter, I share a few additional gems, reflecting on how I incorporated the lessons into my life. Perhaps you will find a way to make them work in your life too! Any time you need a dose of a particular pearl of wisdom, I hope you will pick the book up again and quickly find the encouragement you need.

Mother's Work

Chapter 1

Purpose

The art of mothering is to teach the art of living to children. —Elaine Heffner

Back when I was in graduate school, I helped organize an alumni conference where I heard a panel speaker say, "If you don't know where you're going, any road will take you there." That spoke to me, because I love a plan. In fact, many of my friends from back then teased me about being rigid and obsessed with keeping my work in well-organized folders. Even a few years after graduation, they asked about my folders. They'd probably be surprised to know that they are all of out of order today. And I'm all good with it!

Bringing children into the world moves that kind of stuff to the backburner, at least it did for me. Number one, there's so little TIME. On the other hand, throwing caution to the wind or flying by the seat of my pants is not a comfortable way of life for me either. Sure, I had tried to loosen up some and become a little more adventurous prior to settling down and starting a family. Still, at my core, I need to know what I'm doing and exactly *why* I'm doing it. Slowly but surely, I had to satisfy my yen for purpose and meaning and ease a little bit of that organization back into my life. Early on, I was operating in survival mode. I REALLY was just trying to make it through the day. Every day, I had to do 10 diaper changes, track feedings, wipe noses, and play -- TIMES 2. Sometimes, I was "fun Mommy" and there were lots of smiles and giggles, but other days, I had a short fuse. It became apparent that the lack of purpose sprang from a lack of balance. I woefully neglected my self-care, including healthy eating and fitness. I carved out very little time for things I enjoyed doing like reading, listening to grown-up music, and having long chats with friends. Aside from sleep being an afterthought, my energy was sapped by a diet loaded with carbs and sugars. Thankfully, a nutritionist got me back on track with mindful eating. I also found moments in my day to read an article or make a quick phone call to a girlfriend .

Mother's Work

Wisdom from my own mother, books, and parenting classes, helped crystallize my purpose. In the beginning, I already understood it was my job to teach my children how to move through the world, given all that I had been blessed to learn, such as skills, values, and life lessons. Along the way, I gained additional nuggets of wisdom that helped shape my parenting philosophy.

As I studied the principles of positive discipline when my sons were young, I came away with a distinct, spiritual sense that parenting was my ministry. Adding ministry to my job description forever changed how I envisioned parenting my sons and magnified who I was parenting them for: God and His glory. I attribute another nugget gained during that time to a statement I read to the effect that, children long to be "known." Following the example of God's relationship to me, I committed to getting to know my children. I wanted to learn: heart (intent and desire), head (mind), and hands (actions and tendencies). I aspired to meet them where they were at every stage, not only building them with instruction and discipline, but also caring, connection, and encouragement. This approach felt right as we helped our son overcome his developmental delays. I will share more about that journey in the next chapter on Faith.

Armed with purpose, I was now able to tune out busybodies and naysayers and tune *in* to my children.

Mother's Work

This included eliminating nickname suggestions and pop-up visits as well as standing firm on rules like no kissing my babies on their hands and faces!

As I looked ahead, FAR into the future, my fervent hope was, that at the end of their formative years with me, my sons would be confident, capable, and compassionate; meaning they would value and respect themselves and others, possess useful skills and abilities, and care deeply enough to use those gifts to contribute to the well-being of others as well as themselves. I must also add that as a mother raising black sons, I felt it was imperative that my husband and I train them to be confident and effective communicators while they were young, so they could advocate for themselves when we were not around. I was convinced my concerns were valid back then, but studies in more recent years confirmed my instincts, as they point to implicit bias among educators, healthcare providers, and other professionals when it comes to black children, especially black boys.

It's no secret among racial minorities that when you differ from the norm, people often make snap judgments about you and your potential, but for black children, it can start *ridiculously* early.

According to the 2013-2014 Civil Rights Data Collection (CRDC) conducted by the Department of

Education among public schools and school districts in this country[1]:

- *Black preschool children are 3.6 times as likely to receive one or more out-of-school suspensions as white preschool children.*
- *Black boys represent 19% of male preschool enrollment, but 45% of male preschool children receiving one or more out-of-school suspensions.*

As I concentrated on getting to know my sons, who are fraternal twins, I quickly learned that they are very, very different. Whereas my older twin, Matt, was super-laid back and keenly observant, Zach dove into life headfirst. He laughed hard and cried hard with high energy all the time. Fortunately, he slept hard too! One thing that I knew, though, was that there were benefits to the temperaments and tendencies that both boys came into the world with, and I was eager to channel them in ways that would serve them well as individuals.

Purpose is a great place to start in parenting because, it turns out, children are born seeking purpose. In fact,

---

[1] 2013-2014 Civil Rights Data Collection: A First Look (New Release for 2016), U.S. Department of Education, page 3, www.ocrdata.ed.gov

Mother's Work

they are desperately seeking purpose and desperately in need of our guidance to shape it. This idea is examined thoroughly in one of my favorite parenting books, *Children: The Challenge: The Classic Work on Improving Parent-Child Relations – Intelligent, Humane, and Eminently Practical,* by Rudolf Dreikurs, M.D., and Vicki Soltz, R.N. The authors describe the child's motivation as follows:

"Since the child is a social being, his strongest motivation is the desire to belong. His security or lack of it depends upon his feeling of belonging within the group. This is his basic requirement. Everything he does is aimed at finding his place.[2]

Our children come here sensing they have a place or a purpose for being here and they set out to figure out what it is. As our children set out to find their place and purpose, their approach is often unsophisticated and unproductive, conflicting with the norms of the family. When I talk about this with parents, I ask them to think back to their childhood and imagine what it would be like to be the new kid on the block. As they tentatively explore their new neighborhood, they happen upon a large crowd of children whose

---

[2] Rudolf Dreikurs, M.D.; Vick Soltz, R.N.; (New York, NY: Plume, an imprint of New American Library, a division of Penguin Books USA Inc., 1987; originally published by Hawthorn Books, 1964)

attention is drawn to an activity in the center of a circle. As they move closer, the new kid sees everyone else is watching a game being played. It's a game the new kid has never seen. He has no idea of the rules and the other children are too engrossed in the game to take a moment to explain it to him. Just as he settles in to his spot to watch, one of the children playing turns around and yells, "Sub!" As this child eyes the crowd looking for a suitable candidate, he points at the new kid and says, "You're in!" But wait, he just got here! Well, that's how our children feel in some situations. They're expected to know the rules of the game when they haven't been coached. That's our job. That's our purpose. It's up to us to position them to win in the game of life.

Taking the time to understand them and their unique dispositions helped me detect changes in the pace of Matt's development. He was a very loving and huggable child, and quiet. He laughed and babbled as babies do, but he could do something else – sing. I sang and hummed a lot around the boys. Zach was indifferent, but Matt imitated me, with perfect pitch. Suddenly, at around 13 months, all of those sounds stopped. I also noticed that he didn't respond to me when I redirected his behavior. It appeared that he was ignoring me, but I was certain that wasn't his nature. With their new independence as walkers, both boys were off and running, literally. When I called Zach to come back or stop what he was doing, there was a split second where I could see he heard me, even if he didn't heed my instructions. With Matt, I didn't see that moment of recognition; he didn't miss a step as he ventured off. Even if he was inclined to keep going, he wouldn't ignore me. That much I knew. A little experiment with clanging pots and pans confirmed our suspicion that Matt wasn't actually hearing us. A visit with our pediatrician confirmed this and Matt was treated for fluid in his ears. Our doctor told us the speech and singing should return, but they didn't. We then had Matt tested and started taking him to see a speech and language therapist. Our pediatrician commended us for noticing these red flags when we did because it would have been very easy to dismiss his subtle behavior as defiance or willfulness. Knowing Matt's nature made all the difference and would have implications going forward.

Visits to the speech therapist, and later an occupational therapist, soon became part of our weekly routine. At home, I created visual aids to supplement the hard work Matt was doing at his appointments. This benefitted both boys. I made a wall calendar and attached pictures of the people they would see, the activities they would do, and the places they would go each day. (Never underestimate the power of a mom with a Polaroid camera and Velcro®!) They knew what to expect and seemed to take comfort in that, most days. I have to say I took comfort in the routine as well. What routine meant for me was that I knew what time I could expect to go "off the clock."

Mother's Work

There are definitely many joys of being a stay-at-home mom, but if you're not careful, the days go on and on and you can burn out.

Getting clarity on this notion of my purpose as a parent and moving beyond day-to-day survival mode was life-changing for me. It kept me on task amidst the boys' meltdowns and tears. Whereas before, I tried out a brand-new approach following a particularly rough day, now I'd think about what happened and consider what I could change, but honestly, if I felt I was going in the right direction, I doubled down and tried again. Consistency provides security for young children, even when we are helping them stretch and grow beyond their comfort zone. In business school, I learned "cash is King" and at home with my boys, I decided "consistency is Queen." I became the same mom every day. I think even today, they will tell you that there aren't too many surprises when it comes to my position on most issues.

I remember an amusing conversation a mom recounted that reinforced my thinking about how important it is to be consistent in parenting. As a stay-at-home mom of two, she relayed that she was trying to set up routines and boundaries with her children, while her husband was away at the office or on extended travel for work. Without warning, her husband would walk into a situation with the girls and hand down a decision about it and walk away. He may have had good intentions, but very often he didn't have context and his decision wasn't aligned with the boundaries the mom had already established. More often than not, it had to do with the mood he was in at the moment. She likened what he was doing to "drive-by" parenting wherein the impact on whomever was present was random vs. on purpose or purposeful.

As I took a more purposeful approach to parenting my boys, I felt that my interactions with them became more respectful and affirming of them as individuals. They weren't subject to how much sleep I got the night before or the mood I was in. The focus was on what needed to happen that day or the situation we were in. I was modeling for them how to act with purpose.

It was during that first year that I first heard someone sum up parenting this way: "the days are long, but the years are short." That message encouraged me, and strengthened my resolve to be more purposeful in parenting the boys. I didn't want to feel so overwhelmed that I couldn't enjoy them. I do look back wistfully, and wish I enjoyed them a little more, but I think I wrung out as much pleasure as I knew how at the time. Please, if you are in the season of raising young children, take that sentiment to heart and pour into them what you can while you can. The time *definitely* goes by faster than you think.

Gems From My Journey

- 💎 Get very clear about your values and priorities and walk in your vision.
- 💎 Children seek purpose. Give them space to find it.
- 💎 Tune into your children. Provide the structure they need to develop self-control.
- 💎 Parent for the long term. Be thoughtful and consistent, not random.
- 💎 Operating in purpose affirms your children and provides a living example of how it's done.

Mother's Work

Chapter 2

Faith

Behind every young child who believes in himself is a parent who believed first. – Matthew Jacobson

Faith has always been the bedrock of my existence. I am so grateful for my family's commitment to a Christian upbringing for us children. Both of my parents came from families that were strongly rooted in the church, though my mother was more deliberate about seeing that we got there. She was a psychiatric nurse and sometimes had to work on weekends, but she arranged for us to attend with our friends, if we could not attend as a family. I also have very fond

Mother's Work

memories of attending church and Bible School during my summers in North Carolina visiting my grandparents, aunts, and uncles. I even used to accompany an uncle who was a deacon to church meetings, revivals, and riverside baptisms! As a result of these outings, I became reasonably well-versed in the Bible and the old hymns. My memories of those songs provided consolation during challenging moments in the years ahead. Surely, there were times as a student and young adult when I was more distracted with life and less disciplined than I should have been, but my connection to Christianity had long roots that never let me stray too far from my faith.

My faith was infused with extra steam shortly after our boys turned a year old. As I shared, it was at that time when we discovered that Matt was experiencing developmental delays. Once we lined up the support that he needed and settled into that way of life, I needed some inspiration to anchor me for what was becoming a journey to the unknown. I went back to my foundation, the Word of God.

Despite what doctors were saying, I saw much hope and potential in our son. He was keenly observant, highly empathetic, and meticulous about organizing his toys. I could almost see his mind working, even if he wasn't ready to tell me what he was thinking. I said, "I don't know if he'll be a lawyer or a landscaper, but whatever he does, he'll be the best around." I believed it then and still do. This reflection led me to: 1 Corinthians 2:9 which says, "But as it is written: 'Eye hath not seen, nor ear heard, neither have entered into the heart of man the things which God hath prepared for them that love Him.'" I reasoned that this was just the beginning, and it was no time to be discouraged. I would continue to pray for guidance and trust that the outcome would exceed my imagination. That has certainly been the case.

Because we had two boys, I felt like I needed two spiritual guideposts. I was led to Romans 8:28 which reads, "And we know that for those who love God all things work together for good, for those who are called according to His purpose." As we travelled our path with the boys, it often felt like we had to go the long way around (i.e., more time, more money, more work, etc.) just to get to the same spot as other folks, but I would reflect on this verse and know that I had to trust that our journey was the right one for *us*. My mother used to tell me when I was younger not to be envious of what other people had or experienced because I didn't know the price they paid or what they had been called to do with their blessing, and I never forgot that.

Part of the unique journey we traveled with our sons took them to separate schools for what we did not realize would be most of their childhood. This idea of siblings not attending the same school was a little foreign for me as well as my husband. Logistically, this wasn't always easy, but there were some benefits for the boys. They were each able to learn and grow in academic environments that served them best, with extra support in one instance and more rigor in the other. They benefitted socially as well because they were able to operate on their own turf without being compared to each other.

Separate schools meant separate school administrators for us to deal with and separate extracurricular activities to manage. When the boys were young, they learned how to play basketball in our county's recreation league. They ignited my interest in the sport and I dreamed of their playing on the same basketball court in high school. How was that going to happen if they didn't attend the same school? Or play in the same athletic league? And to top it off, Matt wasn't as crazy about basketball as Zach was, so there was no guarantee that he'd still be playing when they got older. Let me point out here that I was the only one who cared about all of this. I believe it stems from my own regret over not playing high school basketball, despite being practically promised a spot because of my height. I suppose I figured having my children play would ease my heartache. In my mind, their playing together would have been icing on the cake, but it was my cake, not theirs.

Mother's Work

They didn't attend the same high school, and their school competed in different athletic leagues, but things have a way of working out. For some reason, the coaches of the two schools decided they'd have the teams play each other and scheduled a game when our sons were in 10th grade. This was totally unexpected. My husband and I sat in opposite spectator sections for the first half, and high-fived each other on the way to the opposite side for the second half. The boys had not played at the same time during the first half of the game. I wondered if my dream was going to come true. Matt's coach did not realize that he had a brother on the other team, but one of his teammates told him. The coach then put Matt in at the same time that Zach was playing in the second half. My dream was realized and here's the proof!

Mother's Work

Of course, we had the dilemma of only having one team winner, but honestly, we felt our family had won. I had every reason to believe that this could never happen, but I just chalked it up to one of those moments of encouragement God gave me along the way to keep believing and keep on going. Delayed is not denied!

There have been other shining moments when my faith has been rewarded just when I needed a jolt of encouragement; a sign that God was listening. One such flash of light appeared in 2014. I felt deep inside that I wasn't moving in the purpose God had laid out for me and that I needed to expand my platform. I allowed the grievances in my head to take the stage in an intense sort of self talk. Suddenly, as if I turned off the faucet, I had nothing more to say. Exhausted, I prayed and told God I needed a breakthrough and then decided to take a nap. About 30 minutes into it, my phone rang. I considered letting the call go to voicemail, but *something* made me answer. A local radio station had contacted the non-profit group I worked with and wanted a parenting expert who could talk about the life-changing impact of teen pregnancy; AND they wanted to hear from a black parenting expert. The station needed to confirm immediately, so I had to call right away if I wanted the opportunity. I had NEVER been on radio, though I grew up on talk radio because my father was an avid listener. I was *verrrry* nervous, but success rewards the brave, right? I seized that moment, and do you know that station asked me to come back a month later? I was a guest on the morning show to give back-to-school tips for parents.

Within a few weeks of that, a connection I had made on LinkedIn many months before reached out and asked for a meeting. She coached women entrepreneurs and wanted to know more about what I did. That meeting was *pivotal* in launching my career in radio. As a footnote to my discussion of what I did, I said something like, "Oh yeah, I recently did a couple of radio interviews; that was fun." She asked, "Wait, you're on the radio? I said, "*Welllllll*, I've been on the radio twice." She went on to tell me that she had a radio team with women who were experts in their fields and that she had always wanted to do a show on parenting. I decided I had nothing to lose by giving this a try. She had me join her on the next episode of her own show and we launched mine three months later. I was originally going to co-host with another awesome woman, but four months into it, she stepped down to focus on her company. This became a baptism by fire. I had to shift into the role of securing the guests and shaping the personality of the show. My platform was indeed expanding, and quickly. This was a moment. For. Sure.

More recently, my faith was bolstered by another of my favorite passages in the Bible, 2 Kings 4:2, which recounts the story of a widow with two sons and her

Mother's Work

encounter with Elisha. She cried out to him that her husband was dead and that their creditors expected to be paid. She feared they would take away her sons as slaves since she had no money to pay them. Elisha responded in part, "Tell me what do you have in your house." The widow told him she had nothing, except a small jar of olive oil. He told her to go out to her neighbors and round up all the empty jars she could and bring them back to the house. When she had followed his instructions, he then told her to go into a room with her sons and round up all the empty jars she could find. She kept pouring until ALL of those jars were filled! Elisha then directed her to go out and sell the oil, pay off her family's debts, and live on the rest with her sons.

How often do we look around and *think* we lack resources to accomplish our goals? I know I am often guilty of this. At the beginning of 2019, despite almost 15 years in parent education, I wasn't sure what I had to fuel the next leg of the journey in my field. Just three months earlier, I'd had such high hopes. It was Fall 2018 and my sons had started college, so I was ready to ramp up my work with parents and families, and restart this book. With the exception of my radio show, I had eased up over the previous two years on pursuing speaking engagements and other activities that certainly would have helped move me forward. I wanted to be focused and extra-present, to help our sons succeed in those last years in high school. It was also a nostalgic time as I reflected on how far my sons had come. I'm glad I savored those moments. Besides, I couldn't exactly justify going out and speaking to parents about how to be engaged with their children and help them meet life's challenges if I wasn't doing the same for my own.

Here I was, ready to jumpstart my comeback, when something unexpected happened -- my mother became VERY ill. I was devastated. I felt led to drop everything and devote my time to closely monitoring her care instead of my work, but unlike before, I felt God telling me, "I want you to figure out how to do **BOTH**." This was something I struggled with in the past and I don't think I'm different from other entrepreneurs. When major life events happen, you **immediately** think you have to STOP what you're doing. Building a business can already be scary, and any distraction can become an excuse not to try anymore. I was going to try to respond differently this time. Every day when I visited the hospital, I took my laptop. If my mother was resting, I got plenty of work done. If not, I attended to her and focused on making her comfortable. And you know what? As she began to improve, Mom was quite proud and interested in what I was doing. For years, I had a running joke with her that I would be famous one day. I proclaimed that I would even be a guest on the Oprah Winfrey show and I would bring her along. That never happened and, of course, Oprah no longer has her daily show. At the same time, it meant a lot to Mom to see me recognized as a parent educator as she often

Mother's Work

complimented me on the way I was raising my children. She had frequently accompanied me to tapings of my radio show and liked hearing me speak to parents. She was glad to see that I was still able to keep at it. And so it went, for **FIVE** months, until she was able to go home in early 2019.

By then, I had been nominated by a dear friend for the 2019 District of Columbia Mother of the Year® award, sponsored by American Mothers, Inc. American Mothers, Inc. is a nonpartisan, non-profit organization with a mission to "harness the power of maternal energy to make a positive impact in the world."[3] The organization, which celebrates mothers by naming state honorees and a National Mother of the Year®, supports mothers and children through education, advocacy, and grants. They also empower moms to become leaders in their communities and help them forge connections through its collaborative network. American Mothers, Inc. owns the trademark to "Mother of the Year" and is the official sponsor of Mother's Day.

As amazing as all of that sounds, I must tell you that I almost declined the nomination because I just couldn't see how I could add it to my plate. I had to submit a

---

[3] "Our Mission", American Mothers Inc., https://www.americanmothers.org/who-we-are/

portfolio which allowed me to showcase not only my experiences as a mother, but also as a parent educator. Assembling those elements proved to me that, like the mother who had encountered the prophet Elisha, I had a lot "in the house." I was excited to be selected as the honoree for the Washington, DC Metro Area! At a time when I was feeling discouraged, it felt good to be recognized by such an amazing network of mothers from around the country. I saw this not as an opportunity to boast or hold myself out as superior to other mothers, but simply encouragement from God about how I handled my personal journey and a testament to the work of my **own** mother. It was one of the best moments of my life to have her be well enough to attend the gala at the national convention with me.

The historic Mayflower Hotel is where all state honorees for Mother of the Year® converged for the 84th Annual Convention of American Mothers, Inc. One of the highlights of the convention for me was settling in to listen to the 3-minute speeches we were all required to give. Members of the organization, along with family and friends, were in the audience waiting to hear from us. Our theme was "America, this is your mother speaking…" I had spoken before audiences many times before, but this time was very different. I had never publicly shared a story so close to my heart. I was only up there for a few minutes, but I consider it the speech of my life. It would be the first time I spoke in a public forum about our family's challenges guiding our son's academic journey from the early years of trial after trial, to the later years of his hard-earned triumph. Here it is:

Imagine...Looking up from your schoolwork and overhearing your teacher casually say to a colleague, "THOSE kids aren't going to college." My middle schooler rushed home, and asked me urgently, "Mom, I'm going to college, right??" My. Heart. Sank.

America, this is your Mother speaking. YOU can go to college if you want to!

From that day forward, WE started planning. I told his teacher, "Maybe he will go and maybe he won't, but it's NOT up to you."

My son got to work. He had a vision for himself.

Of course, this wasn't the first time someone had cast doubt on my son's potential...

"Your son has pervasive developmental delays. I'm very sorry." A doctor's assessment of MY little boy. His preschool teacher affirmed this, and added, "He's ALWAYS going to be like this."

America, this is your Mother speaking. Speak LIFE in to the heart of your child – He's <u>listening</u>.

We got help for our son – speech therapy, occupational therapy, gymnastics...

Our son got to work. He went <u>mainstream</u> in middle school. He SURVIVED Biology with the amazing

Ms. Avila*. Genes, chromosomes….and PUNNETT squares? **Nailed it!**

And still later, "He can go to our auto repair program!" Now, I think we can all agree – every 5,000 miles, a good mechanic is a good friend! Problem here…my son never <u>said</u> he wanted to be a mechanic.

America, this is your Mother speaking. NO child has to be what he doesn't want to be. Especially when he's willing to <u>work</u> for his dreams.

Our son PULLED A 3.5 GPA, while playing football – earning top academic honors at the state and regional levels. And HERE are his admission letters to college! (Four!)

*America, we have roughly **5 thousand, 3 hundred** colleges in this country. **I believe** all children should be taught, **and treated** as if they have aspirations to go…And given room to make it happen, if they want to. I want that for your child, your child, and EVERY child.*

*Name changed to protect privacy.

It was just a three-minute speech, but in crafting it, I had to go back and sift through some heavy feelings and relive some moments where, emotionally, there was little fuel left in the tank. I was really running on faith (and sometimes, fumes). It felt freeing to say those words out loud. Even today, I pray that message encourages someone. For more about my experience at the convention, see Appendix A for a reprint of my blog recounting the experience.

For the past 7 years, I have had the pleasure of participating in an international Bible study group with women in my local area. One year, it was particularly enlightening to study Moses and his mission to lead the Israelites out of Egypt. You are likely familiar with their many trials in the wilderness. It's amazing how they repeatedly grew impatient, and began grumbling, before slipping into disobedience. This usually occurred very soon after experiencing God's provision, healing, and indeed, His presence with them. What also fascinates is the sheer number of times the laws were restated, in great detail, during this journey. Frankly, it seemed necessary because they kept faltering. The new generation had not witnessed those early acts of grace and the elders who had weren't acting like it. This all reminded me that we must be intentional in speaking our faith and values to our children and in living those words out loud. Deuteronomy 6:6-9 makes it clear how seriously we must take this task:

And these words I command you today shall be in your heart. You shall teach them diligently to your children, and shall talk of them when you sit in your house, and when you walk by the way, and when you lay down, and when you rise. You shall bind them as a sign on your hand, and they shall be as frontlets between your eyes. You shall write them on the doorposts of your house and on your gates.[4]

As philosopher and theologian Albert Schweitzer said, "Example is leadership." Young children are sponges, soaking up what they hear us say and see us do. One day, I got confirmation in an amusing way that our boys were listening to us. Occasionally, they would lobby for permission to do or have something that we didn't allow. They would say, "Well, <insert friend's name> gets to do it, why can't we?" In one of my parenting classes, I learned that instead of disparaging what the friend's parents allowed, it was better to say, "That's okay in your friend's family. It's just not what we do in ours." I guess we must have said it OFTEN. On this particular day, our son was relating a story about one of his favorite classmates, "Mark." He said, "Mark's parents don't let him sleep in the car." We were somewhat friendly with Mark's parents, so we doubted that was true and said, "You probably misunderstood that. We're sure they wouldn't have a problem with him sleeping in the car." Guess what Matt said next? You got it: "Mom, it's not ok in their family, but it's ok in ours." Ah, they *do* listen. I pray that I have been effective in modeling my faith and that they will practice it as emphatically as Matt was

---

[4] The Holy Bible, English Standard Version, Crossway, a publishing ministry of Good News Publishers, 2001

in calling me out at that moment. It's up to them to take that faith walk the rest of the way.

Gems From My Journey

- ❖ Center yourself with a system of beliefs that are anchored to the core of your being.
- ❖ Practice your faith consistently.
- ❖ Live your faith out loud.
- ❖ Pass your faith on to your children.

Chapter 3

Courage

As a mom, I've faced many moments of truth that called for me to rise up and be courageous for the sake of my children and the sake of my family. One of the earliest came when my children were less than a year old. We were trying to find a nanny to help me care for the boys after I had launched a marketing and sales consulting company. We were working with an employment agency that would send over candidates for us to interview. I had received the application for one who I thought would be a great fit for our family. Her name was "Alberta," she was in her late 20s, and originally from Ghana. We interviewed her and she was very pleasant to talk to. She was gentle and loving

Mother's Work

with the boys – this was going to work out...we hoped. I have to add here that while we thought we had found the right person, there was one thing that didn't sit just right with me. The photo of Alberta included with the application seemed a little dubious. The lady we interviewed, who identified as "Alberta," looked a bit different to me, but I couldn't put my finger on what the difference was. Nevertheless, we let her start the first week. I was familiar with her commute, and I was initially a little worried about her making it to work promptly as she didn't have a car, but she was always on time. She got right to work, caring for the boys efficiently and lovingly. Heck, she was even singing to my boys. Meanwhile, I had to go to the agency to sign some additional paperwork. I was given more personnel forms which included another photo of Alberta. A sense of foreboding came over me. Now, I was almost sure this was not the lady working in our house. You don't know how hard we tried to find the right person for the job and Alberta was perfect! So perfect, I was even doing mental and emotional gymnastics trying to make this make sense. I told myself things like, "Well, *whoever she is*, she's very kind to the boys. She's lightened the load for us. We can breathe easier now." Rationalization -- I know! Don't judge me. At least we didn't leave her alone with the boys that first week. My mother was there. When I returned home from the agency visit and walked into the kitchen, I casually tossed the paperwork on the counter to see how my mother would react. She immediately confirmed my suspicions when she asked, "Oh, who's she?" Of course, I knew all along what I had to do. And if there was any doubt, my baby boy made it quite clear. Shortly, after I came home, I placed him on the changing table for a new diaper and he locked eyes with me. I could feel him saying, "I'm counting on you, Mommy." I immediately contacted the agency and of course, the agency owner assured me that Alberta was who she said she was. I told him Alberta couldn't come back and that we needed a refund immediately. When I picked it up a day or so later, the owner said they had lost all contact with Alberta, and with the man claiming to be a relative who helped her with the application. I would later learn from another mom that her family had had a similar bait-and-switch experience. To top it off, the nanny in question had recently been released from prison and hadn't disclosed that little detail. Funny enough, my friend is actually the wife of a high-profile public figure, and had all manner of resources available to prevent something like this. If it could happen to them, I reasoned, it could happen to me. Not sure Alberta was a criminal, but I suspect that her relative hatched this scheme to help her and others in the family find work. I'd love to say we were able to find someone else right away, but it took a beat for us to find the right person to care for our boys and we had the patience to wait.

Not long after we got the childcare issue settled, those two little guys decided to get up and start running, and usually in two different directions. It kept me fit and

Mother's Work

trim, but this chaos couldn't last forever – a sister was tired! It was time to establish boundaries and instill some discipline. My early attempts, like calling out the gentle "No-no-no" were getting me nowhere. With a little trial and error, things became easier, but things got interesting once I start taking those parenting classes I told you about. In short order, I realized the amount of courage this aspect of parenting was going to take.

Some folks might wonder why a parent needs to be courageous to establish discipline. Just tell them what they must do and what they better not do, or else. Right. A parent certainly can do those things, but it's exhausting if you've got to do that all day, year in and year out. How long can you keep that up? More than that, it's suffocating for the child, who is capable of learning how to behave and of learning the consequences of his behaviors. Parents have to be willing to take that time to teach and allow time for the lessons to stick. It takes patience and courage to resist the urge to lay down the law and swiftly punish any infractions. It makes us feel like we're not in charge, after all, and that things are just going to spiral out of control. We want to feel like we're in control at all times as parents. We don't have *complete* control of any other situations or any other people, but somehow we do expect to have it with our children. Why? Mostly, because they're little, but also because we know more than they do.

After thinking all this through, I reasoned since I know more, why not *teach them* more rather than boss them around more or punish them more. Insights gained in my parenting classes and books that I read allowed me to take a few courageous steps:

1. *Examining my motives.* Was my way necessary or did it simply make life easier and more convenient for me? I had to consider how my child was experiencing the situation. Perhaps he was afraid or felt unprepared for it. Heck, maybe he was hungry or sleepy and that's why he was uncooperative. Taking a moment to better understand what was going on with my child as well as what my investment was in the desired outcome often made a world of difference.

2. *Considering my own upbringing.* We all have experiences from our childhood we bring with us to the parenting game. Some of it is useful for our own parenting journey. Other aspects of it? Not so much. It takes courage and compassion to examine it. We don't want to feel like we're second-guessing our own parents. If we do choose a different approach, we might feel like we are dishonoring them. I had to realize that my children were not exactly like me and they certainly were not growing up in the same era, which meant I had to make adjustments that served my family now. I'm sure my parents did the same. I'm not saying this was easy for me, though. I can't tell you how many times I thought, "I would

NEVER have gotten away with this when I was growing up."

Essentially, these first two steps are about self-examination. When the boys were young, I read an excellent book for black parents entitled, *Stickin' To, Watchin' Over, and Getting' With: An African American Parent's Guide to Discipline*. The authors addressed the importance of self-knowledge for parents, saying, "A parent without adequate self-knowledge is like a gardener without garden tools. They may have the ability, but they have to work twice as hard to get half as much results."[5]

3. *Sacrificing short term peace for long term growth.* When you take the long-term view toward the habits and traits you're trying to develop in your child, you have to deal with turmoil and tantrums in the short term. When I speak to parents, I like to say, "You can pay now or you can pay later, but you gotta pay." There's no way around it when it comes to shaping your children's behavior. You have to press on even if one of you is unhappy. Think about it. Would they have ever learned to walk if you hadn't insisted they keep practicing after many frustrating falls?

---

[5] Howard C. Stevenson, Gwendolyn Davis, and Saburah Abdul-Kabir; Stickin' To, Watchin' Over, and Gettin' With: An African American Parent's Guide to Discipline, pg. 27, Jossey-Bass of John Wiley & Sons, Inc., CA 2001

4. *Saying No, or Yes, with purpose and confidence.* Before I took time to think about my true motives for the instructions I gave my sons, I would find myself waffling on my decisions. Once I had clarity about what really *needed* to happen under the circumstances, I felt more confident. Communicating this to the boys became easier. I also had the courage to make corrections if I found I had made a bad call. Having worked through this myself, I now heartily advise parents to give up the idea that their children will always follow their instructions eagerly. Given your 25 – 30-year head start, if you and your children agree on everything, someone's not acting their age and it's YOU.

5. *Taking time to teach instead of taking over.* This was usually easier said than done. It seemed I was perpetually in a rush to get something done or get somewhere. I learned to stop and invest the effort in helping the boys become more independent. Teaching them simple tasks of self-care and managing their own belongings as soon as they were able allowed me to breathe and think. Of course, it made them feel confident and capable after overcoming initial challenges before they mastered the new skills. And it lightened the load for us parents. Young children usually have a keen desire to help. We took advantage of that spirit and energy and continued to teach them how to get things until they left the house. They were surprised to see some of their classmates doing laundry for the first time when they went off to college!

6. *Allowing the boys to make choices.* Again, this feels like giving up control. However, I learned it was wise to let them know they had more control over what happened to them than they thought. Making a link between their actions and their outcomes was eye-opening for them. I can't say they *always* made the best choices as a result of this newfound wisdom, because you know they had to test the waters every now and then. Often there were great outcomes as a result of their choices. For instance, Zach made a vacation suggestion when he was about nine. We followed through on it and had an amazing time. When the boys decided they wanted to have a dog, we let them do the research on breeds and breeders and make the selection. Going on 10 years, I think we all agree getting our dog Tori is one of the best decisions ever made for our family!

7. *Stepping back and allowing the consequences to play out.* Occasionally, this was difficult to do, for many reasons. Imagine your family is out at an event and your child misbehaves. The best solution truly might be to leave. Maybe the rest of you are having a good time, but you all have to pay the price and leave. It may be that the appropriate consequence in another situation might cost you *time* AND *money*, and you hate to lose either. Finally, there are occasions where you feel you can't bear to see your child have to live with painful consequences of his own making, even when it could be a valuable lesson. In moments like that, I just offered what I liked to call "news you can use"

– useful information children can use (or not) before taking action. One such occasion arose at a very inopportune time for Zach. The boys were in 8th grade and preparing to apply to different high schools. Good grades would factor into acceptance decisions. Zach was a very good student -- well-read and engaging in class. He was a decent writer, but his teacher wanted to push him and his classmates to another level. He wasn't eager to do it and his teacher let me know that he was running a little behind on the benchmarks for his upcoming research paper. I relayed the message to him as we both knew his grade on that paper would be highly determinant of his final grade in the class. I told the teacher we were going to have to let the chips fall where they may. I wasn't going to help him because he knew what needed to be done. In the end, the paper was acceptable, if not fully illustrative of his ability. Though he did ultimately have his choice of good high schools to attend, that nail-biter experience impressed upon him the level of effort he needed to put in to writing a good paper.

As you can see, these weren't merely theoretical examples for us. I can relate to every one. We packed up and left places we didn't want to leave, forfeited money spent on events or experiences, and looked on as our children have had to make things right after making the wrong choices. It takes fortitude to trust that our children will learn the lessons.

"Smooth seas do not make skillful sailors."
— African Proverb

Along the way, I have sometimes been bolstered by moments when my children have shown real courage. Once when my son was playing on a neighborhood sports team, he got left behind at a park a couple of miles away from our home. He was about 10 years old. When I pulled up to the park, it was dark, and my son was nowhere to be found! Admittedly, I arrived about five minutes late. His brother and I drove through the parking lot and down a neighboring street and STILL no sign of him. I was starting to get angry. I couldn't understand who would leave a child behind without contacting a parent. Couldn't they have waited five minutes? Now I was frantic. Just as I turned back out to the main street, Matt skipped into view, illuminated by the streetlight above him. I asked him why he was out there on the street and how long he had been out there. He explained that he came out of the park to where it was light because he wanted me (or someone who could help) to see him. He told me he knew how long he had been out there because he stopped someone and asked him the time. I was horrified, but quite proud of how bravely he handled himself. He honestly could not understand why I was so upset!

Mother's Work

Here's another little story, rich with valuable lessons learned over time that have given me the courage to parent the unique children God blessed me with:

Ahhh.....I had just settled in with the parents at a birthday party in the park by a creek while Zach played with the birthday girl and their 4th grade classmates. Alas, I was jarred awake from my chill-phoria as this question was loudly asked over the din of shrieks and giggles and immediately following a big...SPLASH: "Who's got the kid in the red shirt?" By now, you have accurately surmised that the parent who had brought the "Kid in the Red Shirt" was indeed...ME!!!! After some quick thinking, and a trip to a friend's nearby home to dry the soggy garments, we were back on the party scene and I could only chuckle as three or four more kiddos subsequently experienced the same fate as my red-shirted one. Yep, they also took the plunge into that creek! Whose idea was it to put a creek in the middle of a birthday party, anyway??

That occasion came to mind as we prepared to send our daredevil off to college, and I feel like it's almost a metaphor of the parenting journey. Think about it --- as our children conquer the trying terrain of growing and becoming, mistakes and missteps happen and before you know it, you get the call, "Whose kid is this?" Just when you're thinking they're in a good place, your relationship is sailing along, and you can breathe a sigh of relief, you've got to get back on your feet, take your place on the sideline and start actively coaching and maybe even retraining. In these moments, you can feel like you've been ignored, defeated, and frankly tasked with a job you're not quite up to. NO other parents have to deal with this stuff, you say to yourself. You're thinking if only your child could act like your niece because that girl is on the ball. Or you're obsessing over how your friend and her son have such a loving, easy relationship. Surely, he doesn't give his mother a moment's worry or trouble. These spectator assessments and comparisons aren't helpful or fair to you and certainly not to your child.

I have a few thoughts for your consideration:

A. The problem you're now facing reared its head when you were around to help. Be thankful for that. It signifies a need your child has or a gap in her knowledge and/or skills. You are there to help her fill that gap. Help her solve *her* problem, so she can take the lead next time when you are not there.

B. Every parent's journey is unique. Each road presents a different set of experiences, lessons learned from those experiences and a resulting outlook that you can never be fully privy to, and one you certainly can't duplicate for your home with different actors in your family movie.

C. You don't know the family's entire journey. You only see snapshots in time, even with close relatives and friends. You don't know how much work they have put in to get things where they are or what it takes for them to maintain harmony at any given moment. You don't know which battles they have decided not to fight, which also shapes the circumstances you are witnessing.

D. The dynamic between every parent and child is unique to them and they each have to learn how to navigate it. It's like how we naturally adapt to a particular dance partner. To get in sync, and stay in sync, we have to consider what our partner is doing and move accordingly, whether we're going with the flow or we want to change that dance a bit. A child's behavior that may drive you crazy could be perfectly acceptable for your sister and her husband. Similarly, what you are willing to tolerate might not fly over at your friend's house.

It takes courage to raise the "kid in the red shirt." It also takes courage to *be* that kid in the red shirt and it's a parent's job to meet him where he is. I knew I had to rise up to that challenge and find ways to nurture a courageous spirit in my son. Moreover, as a child with brown skin, he would require another layer of armor to protect his heart as society turned on him, recategorizing him from cute little black boy to scary black adolescent. This has meant frank conversations about the history of race in America and its current manifestation. When they were younger, we could issue warnings and admonishments about their behavior in the general terms of appropriate behavior. Occasionally, they saw hints that the rules applied differently to other children their age, particularly at school. However, for our children, it was the tragic killings of Trayvon Martin, Jordan Davis, and then Michael Brown, that really opened their eyes and let them see that Mom and Dad weren't trying to ruin the party. Sadly, there have been many more, too many more, to name here. While other families have "The Talk" with their children about sex, black and brown families must have THE Talk about race, particularly, the intersection of race and law enforcement. Against this backdrop, we had to foster courage and hope in our children. And we had to start early.

Once when Matt was in 3rd grade, there was another student who was bigger than he was and who liked to get in his face. He came and told me what was happening. He asked me to call the student's mother. I said, "Nope." He then asked me to talk to the student. I said, "No, he and I get along fine." Matt's eyes grew bigger now as he moved into pleading mode, "Well, are you going to talk to my teacher?" I said, "Nope. You are." I could see the reluctance in his eyes, but I assured him I wasn't going to leave him hanging out there by himself. He walked me through what was going on with the other student. I wanted Matt to spell out what was bothering him and how he wished things could be instead. We role-played a conversation with the other student. Once I saw he felt more comfortable with that exchange, I had him practice approaching the teacher to ask her to set up (and moderate) a meeting for Matt and the other student. I gave him a pep talk on the drive to school and when he got there, he walked to the classroom and made a beeline for his teacher's desk. He told her what he needed while his courage was high. She arranged the meeting and things were resolved. I will readily admit that up to that point, I may have intervened here and there on Matt's behalf in working out social situations. However, something told me that even if it was extra-hard for him, now was the time for him to learn to resolve conflicts on his own. Little did I know how much this experience would pay off. He went on to become such a capable advocate for himself that his teachers often complimented him on that ability throughout the rest of his years in school. We always knew he liked order and decorum. He just needed a little coaching on how to explain that to everybody else.

There have been other instances where our sons have impressed me with their bold and courageous decisions. One instance came when Zach was a junior in high school. He had landed an interview with a popular fast-food restaurant. We admired his drive to earn extra money for himself, but I wasn't too crazy about this particular fast-food chain. At a corporate level, its leaders had taken some political stances on issues affecting black people and other groups that I could not support. In fact, we had stopped patronizing that restaurant chain for a few years leading up to this interview. Nevertheless, I decided not to hinder him in pursuing this opportunity. So proud and excited about this opportunity was he that he decked himself out in his "Sunday best" for the interview, even as his friends advised khakis and a polo would be just fine. He got to the interview and things were going very well. Actually, so well that he was pretty sure he had the job. Just as he and the manager were wrapping up with small talk, he asked, "Can I tell you something? My mother doesn't like this company anymore because…" and he laid it all out. The manager told him she appreciated his candor and explained the franchise concept to him. She assured him that the owners of that particular location held dramatically different political views from the founders. She cited examples of how their policies reflected that. I have to tell you, when he came home and relayed this to me, my response was, "Dude, you were home free! You told her what???" In the end, though, I had to admit that was audacious. I admired him for raising an issue that was concerning to him as well. (Even if he did kinda throw me under the bus.)

As proud as a I am of my own children, I would be remiss if I didn't call attention to the courage of children and youth throughout history. When we think about the change their actions brought about, we can see the value of instilling this attribute of character very early. Let's take the civil rights movement as an example. We all have great admiration for Rosa Parks and the resolute stance she took by refusing to give up her seat to a white passenger on December 5, 1955. What some may not realize is that a 16-year-old named Claudette Colvin had refused to give up *her* seat about 9 months earlier on March 21st that same year. Moving ahead a few years to May 1963, there was the Children's Crusade in Birmingham, AL where black children took to the streets to make their voices heard.

> *[The crusade]was intended to force integration of public spaces and local businesses in the famously segregated city. Although unsuccessful in immediately desegregating the city's public spaces, the Crusade did bring national attention to the harsh realities of Jim Crow laws in the South. Soon after the event, Pres. John F. Kennedy called for a civil rights bill that one year later became the Civil Rights Act of 1964.[6]*

These children stood strong as police confronted them with threats of arrest, police dogs, and fire hoses. In recent years, black youth as well as their elders have

---

[6] London, Grace, "Children's Crusade." 10/06/2017, accessed 09/01/2020.
http://www.encyclopediaofalabama.org/article/h-3944.

rallied under the mantle of the Black Lives Matter movement, which sprang up around 2013 as a rebuke of the violence and systemic racism that black people have faced in the U.S. As police-involved killings of unarmed black men and women escalated, the crowd of activists slowly grew in racial, cultural, and generational diversity; and a new wave of outrage emerged in 2020 following the death of George Floyd as he was detained by police officers in Minnesota. Some may attribute this drive to shock, seething anger, or profound hurt. These certainly might be contributing factors, but I believe their collective response is a testament to their resilience and bravery. Somewhere, they learned their ideas matter and they mustered up the courage to make their voices heard.

And it's working. Awareness of racial injustice experienced routinely by black and brown people has increased exponentially. Businesses, communities, and local officials are taking notice, and in many cases, taking action. This is but a recent example of young people taking a stand over recent years, along with the Standing Rock protest over the Dakota access pipeline and the March for Our Lives movement prompted by the surge in school shootings. Giving children a safe space to pursue challenges, test ideas, and use their voices equips them to bring fresh solutions to tomorrow's nagging problems.

Mother's Work

As I began to apply what I learned early on in parenting classes, I found that much of what I was doing to encourage and foster confidence in my children could easily be applied to me. For example, when one of the boys misbehaved and had to experience an unpleasant consequence like leaving the park early or losing a privilege, I'd usually say something like, "You can try again tomorrow." I always wanted them to look to tomorrow as a fresh opportunity to get things right. Over time, that idea encouraged me as well. Usually, in the evenings after the boys were tucked into bed, I'd debrief the day as I wound down. As is typical human nature, I'd replay the tough moments first – meltdowns, temper tantrums, and spilled milk. Sometimes, it was the boys' fault and other times, I would share with my husband that it wasn't my finest hour. I considered how I could have handled the situation differently and vowed to myself I would try something new the next time. I also reflected on the moments that went smoothly and were enjoyable. I challenged myself to create more of those positive reflections. Ultimately, if I wanted the boys to believe that each new day started with a clean slate, I had to believe it myself.

The courage I built at home with my sons empowered me in other circumstances as well. There was such a moment in my early days as a parent educator when I was co-leading a class based on positive discipline. My co-leader is a real force of energy while I am more reserved and calm, probably because of my family's

Mother's Work

southern roots. Anyway, over time we managed to create a style that provided a well-balanced setting that class participants pointed out before we realized it. By this time, we both had been co-leading classes a few years, though it was only our second time teaching together. This time around, it just happened that in addition to typical child-rearing challenges, about a third of the parents were also wrestling with major life dilemmas; mostly divorces and separation, but also illnesses. You could see, physically, that life was wearing them down. One day, a gentleman (I'll call him "Sam") in our class was scheduled to come in to meet with my co-leader a little early before class to discuss some challenges he had relating to his children. He also needed to neutralize his estranged wife's negative influences. Aside from being a skilled parent educator, my co-leader is also a phenomenal life counselor, which I am sure would have equipped her to have a very rich conversation with Sam. I live a good distance away and traffic in my area can be a real headache, so I always left home very early to ensure I made it to class well ahead of time. As usual, I arrived early that morning, and a few minutes later, Sam came in. We made small talk and he reminded me that he was there to meet with my co-leader. It was unlike her not to be there on time. I knew Sam needed the help my co-presenter could provide, and I KNEW I was not up to tackling this situation. I am willing to bet I PRAYED my co-leader would hurry up and walk through the door any minute. After getting the room set up with still plenty of time before class, I checked my phone and saw a text from my co-leader. She apologized profusely that she had been delayed and there was no way she'd make it there early. She guessed she would likely make it just in time for class. My first thought was to tell Sam he'd have to schedule another time to talk with my co-leader. I was oh-so-close to telling him that, but I knew he needed help. Instead, I explained the situation to Sam and told him I would be willing to talk and try to help him. He said OK. He waded into the conversation by sharing a little background on his past and current family dynamics. Clearly, Sam wanted to repair and strengthen his relationship with his children. Out of nowhere, words started coming out of my mouth as I relayed my thoughts and feelings as an eleven-year-old watching my parents' divorce. I shared how my parents conducted themselves during that time and how they each engaged with me. I described the impact it all had on me, for better and for worse. Throughout the conversation, we also discussed the concepts we were covering in class and how they related to the situation he was facing. At the end of our conversation, he said I had been helpful, and he appreciated my taking time to speak with him.

As the class progressed and my co-leader and I shared more tools and strategies, Sam and the other participants in the class began to feel more confident and appeared lighter and less discouraged. We saw more smiles on the participants' faces. They also engaged more with us and each other. On the last day of class, the parents carried themselves differently, even appearing taller, than when they started class. That is what truly makes this work rewarding. It is about helping parents take heart in the inevitable travails of parenting, and adding instruments to their toolbox to equip them to meet and master those moments. I'm glad that I took that step up to help Sam at the moment he needed my assistance. It has emboldened me to take similar opportunities to pour into the hearts of parents, to ultimately make a positive impact on their children's lives.

The value of courage to be a mom cannot be overstated when you consider that our job, right from the start, is rooted in serving as encourager-in-chief for our children. Early on, we've got to believe for our children before they even dare to do so for themselves. Before we can do that, however, we have to be who we are and own what we do as moms.

A few years back, I had an epiphany that being a mom is certainly enough. As a matter of fact, I saw that a mother's perspective might be exactly what is needed in professional settings, away from my home and family. I had the privilege of participating in a career forum for minority high school students in Charlottesville at the business school I attended. The objective was to get the freshmen and sophomores thinking about careers in business and what it might be like to pursue an MBA. I, along with six other

Mother's Work

panelists, including some alums, were asked to talk about the work we do, our various pathways to the work we do, and how the students might begin to blaze their own trail to a career in business.

Speaking to the students sounded like something nice to do, but I had reservations about accepting the invitation. For starters, I was very busy with work. To complicate matters, the forum date fell during the week I had promised my mother I would take her on a trip to North Carolina and I intended to keep my word. As I hesitated to commit, the host pleaded with me, saying that there was no one else on the panel who did the kind of work I do. Hearing that, I confirmed with the host and told Mom the trip to North Carolina was still on, but we'd have to make a stop first. As always, I had her full support! She packed her bags and was ready to ride.

As I prepared for my intro and thought about ideas I wanted to share concerning my work, I suddenly panicked. I wondered how I would explain what I do to high schoolers in a way that is compelling. At that point, I… was… JUST… a… mom! Sure, I had the nice title of Parent Educator and Consultant; I was even certified, but I was JUST a mom who talked to moms (and some dads) about being a mom or dad and family life… blah… blah… blah…. I was going to be sitting next to a senior official from the World Bank, senior managers in finance and marketing from

Mother's Work

international corporations, and entertainment moguls. Plus, one of the ladies from the Real Housewives franchise was going to be the keynote speaker later that day. What was I doing here? I had had a successful career in marketing, but that seemed like eons ago. Now, I am... just... a ... mom. Well, I got through it. At the end, students were free to ask questions and speak to us personally if they were interested. You know the line for the reality show star was a mile long. And the kids wanted pictures with her too! Still, students also came over to speak with me. They said things like, "I admire what you're doing." Or "People like you are doing important work." One student said he already volunteered with children after school, and he had decided that shaping the lives of children was what he ultimately wanted to do with his life. Wow. I must tell you that my day was made when one young man came up to me, meekly but determinedly, and said, "I liked hearing about what you do for parents and about the things you do with your son. I have learning disabilities, too, and my mother has really helped me," and he smiled broadly and proudly. As he spoke, I studied him; in his eyes, I could see the determination and the practice it probably took to prepare him for such a moment as this. The courage he displayed sharing a little of his story and his struggles with me, a stranger, was incredible to me. I knew right then that no mother is JUST a mom. George Washington said, "My mother was the most beautiful woman I ever saw. All I am I owe to my mother. I attribute all my success in life to the moral, intellectual and physical education I received from her." Barbara Kingsolver proposed, "The strength of motherhood is greater than natural laws." And finally, dear Dr. Maya Angelou declared, "A mother's love liberates." If there is one thing I have come to know for sure, no mother is JUST a mom. Not yours, not mine, not you, not me.

I've found that being a mother calls for us to be brave and vulnerable at the same time. You have to be courageous enough to fail. And willing to put yourself out there again. Every day. I applied this concept outside of parenthood. Take basketball for example. First, I must let you in on a little secret. I'm not a GREAT basketball player. As I said before, I took it up later in life, despite the fact that most people who meet me are convinced I played in school because of my height. Actually, basketball is in my DNA. My mother and aunts played, and I have two female cousins who played at an elite level in the NCAA. What about me? I always tell people that during my childhood, girls' basketball wasn't huge where I lived, and it certainly didn't have prominence on the national stage. This meant that I didn't have any role models my age. That's part of it, but a major factor was that I had already mastered other sports and didn't want to learn another from scratch by the time my growth spurt took off in 9th grade. I didn't want to NOT be good at basketball. I discovered a real love for the game when Michael Jordan came along. At that point, learning to play basketball went on my

Mother's Work

bucket list. Watching my sons play intensified my interest. I took up the game a while back with a league in my neighborhood for women of a "certain age." Taking that step ignited a spirit of courage and desire that extended to other areas of my life, especially business. So much so that I don't make much time to play anymore. I'm sure I'll get back to it, but I am very grateful for the shots I have been making off the court. I win sometimes and sometimes I lose, but I keep putting 'em up. Are you willing to try something new? Level up in your business? Live more courageously? Give it your best shot! Listen – when I co-founded my company, someone told me our message wasn't unique or clever. In January 2018, the U.S. Patent and Trademark Office said otherwise! You've got nothing to lose, but lessons and blessings to gain!

Mother's Work

Gems From My Journey

- Decide to be courageous. Your children are counting on you.
- Be bold and parent the children you have the way they need to be parented.
- Give your children opportunities to build the muscle of courage.
- Make being courageous a habit. You can only impart encouragement for your children from a deep, expanding well of courage within you.
- Be courageous enough to fail. As they say in baseball, "you gotta swing for the wall to win it all."

Mother's Work

Chapter 4

Wisdom

Children don't come with an instruction manual. That means we've got to seek wisdom. It's unbelievable to me that the act of molding and shaping a human being, your precious child, is expected to come naturally to parents. None of us grow up receiving formal instructions on how to be a good parent. Then one day that awesome responsibility is thrust upon us. Some folks think you shouldn't need to read books or take classes to raise children, firmly believing it's not that hard to do. Even I thought it was far easier than it is. I soon came to see, however, that gathering knowledge about parenting wherever you can is no different from making time to learn how to give a

Mother's Work

proper haircut. You might eventually figure out these skills, but how many trials are people going to give you if you don't know the basics? Plus, some mistakes might actually be painful. The same goes for raising children. Your child can survive a bad haircut, but bad parenting is so much harder to overcome. If you need more convincing, check out what it says in the Book of Proverbs:

Proverbs 4:7 - Wisdom [is] the principal thing; [therefore] get wisdom: and with all thy getting get understanding.

Proverbs 8:11 - For wisdom [is] better than rubies; and all the things that may be desired are not to be compared to it.

How might you acquire this wisdom? One approach is to seek counsel from your elders. This might also yield some valuable practices and traditions that you could carry forward in your family. Also, you can try an idea out and if it doesn't feel right for your child, tweak it, or scrap it. You don't have to start from scratch on everything. Save yourself some time! Friends who have more parenting experience can also be a valuable resource. I'll forever be grateful to my friends who passed down an Exersaucer. (For those of you who aren't parents yet, this life-saving contraption sits firmly on the floor and holds an infant upright in a cloth seat with holes that allow the legs to come through. It provides support on the bottom surface as the baby bounces up and down. While there are different variations, all versions have trays or holders for toys.) We bought one more and these Exersaucers kept our boys occupied while I cooked dinner or got some work done around the house. Bonus: all that exercise made nap time a breeze! I sought advice from my friends on more significant concerns, too, but LISTEN -- that little invention saved my sanity! Of course, your pediatrician and other professionals can also provide a wealth of information. Take advantage of it. My pediatrician kept me abreast of the latest medical advancements, books by parenting experts, and best practices in childcare, and always sent me home with valuable materials.

The parenting classes provided another source of wisdom for me. The boys had hit the "teachable twos," and I needed advice on coping with that challenging phase. I also sought ideas on how to nurture and parent our twins as individuals. Positive Discipline, which was the foundation of those classes, put me on the path of bringing out their unique gifts and talents, while preserving that special connection they had as twins. As I mentioned earlier, it's rooted in Adlerian Psychology, which holds that all human behavior can be explained by our desire to meet these key goals: to connect, count, contribute, and care. How we each go about meeting those goals is rather individualized and understanding each son's way of being was key for me. I also found parenting talks and seminars to be helpful over the years.

Mother's Work

Next, tap into your own maternal instincts. When the boys started walking and got their first real walking shoes, I remember having to write their initials on the bottoms, since they were wearing the same size at the time. I asked my stepfather to hand me Matt's shoes and he handed me Zach's shoes. Without looking at the bottom, I told him they were the wrong ones. He asked, "How do you know?" I said I could tell by the way the shoes were shaped from wear. I don't exaggerate when I say I was thoroughly entertained by how each boy moved through life, literally, from head to toe. There are some things you just know about your children. Treasure your maternal wisdom, In my case, it tipped me off to the developmental delays Matt was experiencing.

As life happens, we have many opportunities to pour wisdom into our children. Conversations and lessons shared are priceless. We can also plant the seeds of self-control and water them daily by modeling it along with respect when guiding them. We can have lasting influence in our children's lives – when the grades are less than perfect, when friendships are broken, siblings are squabbling, basketball games are lost, soccer goals are missed, love professed is unrequited… the list goes on. They can learn to exercise wise judgment in these circumstances from us.

Mother's Work

I had an experience when my children were young that made me ever so thankful for wisdom and self-control. I encountered a woman in a parking lot who complained that I had parked too close to her car making it "impossible" for her to get in. My license tag numbers had been called out over the PA system and I immediately rushed to the front of the store. After the store clerk explained the problem, I dashed out to move the car. As I got closer to it, the aggrieved woman ran up behind me and started yelling, "I was about to call the police." That threat hadn't become quite the trigger it has today with white people calling the police on black people for non-urgent matters, but if I hadn't been in a rush to get back home, I might have been willing to let that play out because this woman was totally out of order. I felt like I was dealing with actual child in the midst of a temper tantrum. She punctuated her tirade by calling me a royal [w]itch with a b for parking there. Well, I've got to tell you I could have gone in several different directions after that comment, but prudence prevailed. This young lady was obviously unstable. I took a deep breath, considered my family waiting for me, and said calmly, "At least you recognize I'm the Queen." I then proceeded to move my car.

Later, my alter ego was telling me, "You are slipping. You had at least a foot [in height] on her, plus you know tae kwon do. At a minimum, you should have cursed her out." I have to admit I was surprised at my composure because my temper has gone from 0 to 60

Mother's Work

seconds more than a few times in my life. This "child" looked to be in her late 20s, but as I watched her melting down, I could only laugh at her and think, "Is that all you've got? I'm a mom, I know how this game goes." It brought to mind the scripture, 1 Corinthians 13:11, "When I was a child, I spoke as a child, I understood as a child, I thought as a child: but when I became a man, I put away childish things." As we hear about senseless acts of violence, we come to understand that some people have not put away their childish, irrational ways of handling anger, hurt, and dissatisfaction, and respond with catastrophic results for the rest of us. In the end, we all must make, and live with, our decisions. The sooner our children learn that, the better and safer for all of us.

"Educate your children to self-control, the habit of holding passion and prejudice and evil tendencies subject to an upright and reasoning will and you have done much to abolish misery from their future and crimes from society." – Ben Franklin

Sometimes wisdom tells you the battles aren't worth your time. Other times, you've gotta go in. When it was time to search for high school, Zach wanted to apply to five schools. One of the schools was a favorite of mine with a great reputation, leading edge facilities, but a competitive admissions process. He went for his shadow visit, to accompany a current student to classes for the day, while I was to attend an information session for parents 'and prospective students later in the afternoon. After dropping him off, I along with another black parent, stopped at the information desk for directions to the info session room. The first staffer didn't know the answer, so another came over and asked, "Oh, did you want the brochure for the <name of the remedial program>?" Wow. How did we go from asking for a room number to being offered brochures about the remedial program? Undeterred, we left the area and planned to return for the info session. The administrator described the various aspects of the school, including the honors program. A couple of other parents asked questions, with one white mother asking a ton of questions about the honors program. The administrator spoke glowingly about it, covering every concern. Finally, I, the only black parent to raise her hand, asked a question about admission to the honors program itself, aside from the school. I wanted to know if students applied separately to the honors program or if administrators selected candidates based on the full application to the school? As she prepared to answer my basic question, she prefaced her response with, "Now, you have to understand the honors program is for the BEST of the best students. It's very hard…" Again. Wow. Why didn't the other parents get that preamble? I turned to Zach and said, "I guess you know what you've got to do." He smirked and said, "Yep."

Mother's Work

He applied and got in. Yay. I guess. Next up, it was time for this same school to woo accepted students at a special dinner. We ran into the Admissions Director and she was pleasant enough. When Zach introduced himself, she said, "Yes, I remember. You'll be coming in to our <name of remedial program>, right?" Caught off guard, he says, "Um.... No" Still again. Wow. We moved on to mingle with other parents as well as school administrators. There was small talk with more than a few who assumed he was enrolling as a recruit for their highly-ranked basketball team and asked him about that. I mean he IS tall, but did they have to look so surprised upon learning that he was actually admitted on his smarts alone? As the evening wore on, this school quickly fell out of favor with me. My husband and I sat down with Zach and talked about our overall experience with the school. In the end, it wasn't Zach's first choice either. He took his talents elsewhere and things turned out fine. As Maya Angelou said, "When someone shows you who they are, believe them the first time. " And the fourth time, if you're hard-headed. Trust your maternal wisdom. It doesn't usually fail you. And by all means pass these lessons on to your children.

We are wise to acknowledge our children's wisdom as well. When Matt was about a third of the way into the school year as a 6th grader, we realized his school was no longer the place for him. The students' behavior was getting way out of hand, even for that difficult age. I did not agree with how teachers and administrators were handling that issue. On top of that, I was disappointed in the quality of instruction he was receiving that year. Up to this point, we had assumed he would finish high school there and now, late in the game, we were going to have to look at schools again. After making our rounds of Open Houses and submitting all the applications, it was time for school visits and/or shadow days. I dropped Matt off at one school that I was about 90% sure he'd end up attending. When we got there, we even saw a couple of people he knew. Once he was signed in, I headed off to teach a class. When I got home, I had a message from the Admissions Director asking me to come back a little early, to talk about how the day went. When we sat down for our meeting, she told me that she was in and out of classes, observing Matt and other visitors. She said during one of those check-ins, Matt came up to her and said, "Excuse me. Can you call my Mom? This isn't going to work out." She said she told him she was sure that I wanted him to experience the whole day and asked that he spend a little more time there. She said that if he still wanted to leave when she came back around, she'd call me. She would later tell me that she didn't call me to pick him up because the parent essay we submitted gave her the impression I wouldn't like that. YIKES! I certainly would *not* have been angry, but I do like for Matt to see things through, and I guess she picked up on that. It turned out Matt didn't ask to leave anymore, but when she asked him toward the end of the day how things went, he told her, "These children need a lot of help. This isn't the place for me. Can you call my Mom and tell her to pick me up?" By this time, she knew I was on my way for our meeting, and she relayed that to him.

When we sat down, she asked me if he realized that he already attended a school for students with learning differences. I told her he did, indeed. She went on to say she was surprised at his reaction and that she thought the school would be a perfect match for his learning profile. I told her that I would talk to him about it when we got home, see what his concerns were, and get back to her by the end of the evening. The tricky thing here was that the school required a two-day shadow visit. How in the world was I going to convince the boy that he had to come BACK tomorrow?

A short time later, Matt joined us in the office. We thanked the director for her time and headed to the car. As we made our way home, I asked Matt what he thought about the school. He repeated his position that this school was not the right place for him. He felt that the teachers hovered a little too much around the students and he didn't need that kind of help anymore. I reminded him that wherever he went, he would need *some* support, so why not go there (since I was 90% sure that was where he needed to be). He told me he wanted to go to our neighborhood public school instead. That school was the next and final school on the list for a shadow day. Thanks to the horrendous rush hour traffic, we each had plenty of time to lay out our arguments on this matter. I promised him that we would hold off on the second shadow day for this school and arrange to visit the neighborhood school next. I did reiterate my position that, on paper, the school he'd just visited seemed perfect for him. I also told him that we had to make an agreement that if the neighborhood school was not the right fit, we would be going back to the other school to complete the shadow visit and he would likely end up attending school there. Matt said, "Deal!" and shook my hand. The visit to the neighborhood school went far better than we could have hoped. The school had everything he needed, along with opportunities for him to be more independent and learn alongside kids he knew from our community. Matt did not initially know anything about what the neighborhood school offered or whether it offered what he needed. He did discern clearly what he *didn't* need when he saw it at the other school. This was a big lesson for me about trusting my children's wisdom.

Gems From My Journey

- Seek wise counsel and knowledge.
- Tap into your maternal instincts and trust them.
- Pass wisdom on to your children.
- Kids have wisdom, too.

Mother's Work

Chapter 5

Love & Friendship

You're probably wondering why we've gotten this far in the book and I'm only now focusing on love. The fact is my parenting journey began with love and is infused with it, still. It was in love that my children were created and with love that I jumped headfirst into this journey of caring, nurturing, and helping to mold them. Love also shows up in my friendships and the way I engage with my fellow man and woman in my community.

As I reflect on the importance of love and friendship in my journey, I turn to the framework conceived by

Mother's Work

the Ancient Greeks through which they defined 8 types of love. I will talk about five that I found particularly relevant in my life as a mom: eros (passionate love), storge (familial love), philautia (self-love), agape (unconditional love), and philia (friendship). The first and highly crucial examples of love, for children, are usually experienced within their own families and in their own home.

Eros

Eros is sexual or passionate love, and most akin to the modern construct of romantic love. In Greek myth, it is a form of madness brought about by one of Cupid's arrows. The arrow breaches us and we "fall" in love, as did Paris with Helen, leading to the downfall of Troy and much of the assembled Greek army.[7]

In my early childhood, I have some recollection of sensing love between my parents. I remember trips we took together, events we attended, and times spent at home. I can recall the sense of security it provided for me. I can also remember feeling the loss of that sense when their marriage came to an end. However, I am thankful for the love they each showed to me as we

---

[7] Burton, Neel, "These Are the 7 Types of Love", Hide and Seek, Psychology Today. 06/25/2016, accessed 07/05/2020, https://www.psychologytoday.com/us/blog/hide-and-seek/201606/these-are-the-7-types-love.

moved forward from there. As I grew older, I resolved to be *very* thoughtful before getting married and having children, because I wanted our child(ren) to feel nestled within a loving partnership.

Early in my marriage, I remember hanging out in bookstores with my husband on Sunday afternoons. On one occasion, I ran across a miniature book called the *Little Book of Marriage* by Thomas Hesburgh. In it was a quote I made a note of, "The most important thing a father can do for his children is love their mother." The converse is also true and, of course, this maxim should apply to all parents who bring children into their union. It provides the first glimpse of love for children and parents should tend to it intentionally and consistently, even while raising active children. I'll be the first to admit this can be a challenge, but it's worth it. Making time for intimacy, date nights, and getaways keeps things interesting, but just as important are loving, respectful interactions in our home every day. Showing affection, sharing laughs, and tackling problems together, day-to-day, are also great displays of love in action, even in a busy household. I highly doubt our sons will look back years from now and say we were the perfect parents, but I think they would be hard-pressed to say we didn't love each other.

Storge

Storge, or familial love, is a kind of philia pertaining to the love between parents and their children. It differs from most philia in that it tends, especially with younger children, to be unilateral or asymmetrical. More broadly, storge is the fondness born out of familiarity or dependency. Compared to eros and philia, it is much less contingent on our personal qualities.[8]

My mother is very loving and has a great sense of humor. I don't recall her talking about her love for me each and every day, but she showed her love in the way she took care of me. My father was not one to *verbally* express love every day either. I think my parents were both more inclined at that time to show their love by what they did more than what they said. Perhaps it was a generational thing, or the fact that they both grew up in large farming families where there might not have been much time to say, "I love you," but they always knew it was there. In any case, between my parents and our large extended family, I actually felt very much loved.

---

[8] Burton, Neel, "These Are the 7 Types of Love", Hide and Seek, Psychology Today. 06/25/2016, accessed 07/05/2020, https://www.psychologytoday.com/us/blog/hide-and-seek/201606/these-are-the-7-types-love.

Mother's Work

Mom was very often in a pleasant mood, singing and humming around the house when I was little. Older cousins on both sides of the family have often mentioned how much fun she was and how much they enjoyed her when they were younger. At the same time, she liked things in order and expected good behavior. After my parents divorced, she expected us to step up our game on being responsible around the house and in school. By then, she was working various nursing shifts, but still cared well for us and was there when we needed her. Even when I wasn't in her presence, it always felt like Mom was with me. Starting in college, we always had established days for phone calls to check in and make sure all was well. My mother often sent cards and care packages back then. After graduation, I returned home for a few months before moving to Philadelphia to live on my own for the first time. The cards and care packages resumed! A couple of years later, as I headed off to graduate school, I had to make a special request. I wanted to receive a card every Wednesday, because that was about the time of week when I would need extra encouragement to keep grinding through that rigorous program. Of course, I received my weekly card from her on Wednesdays! Every bit of this was love for me.

Without a doubt, it's also good to hear the three words – I love you. Early on, my husband and I had the habit of saying it every day to each other. This practice naturally found its place in our connection and

Mother's Work

interaction with the boys in times of joy and in moments that were less than joyful. When the boys were 4- or 5-years old and *really* beginning to understand more about the consequences of misbehavior, we'd often have them go cool off (similar to taking a time-out) after an incident. They could come back when they felt ready to join the rest of the family. Once they apologized and/or talked about what had happened, we usually hugged them and said, "I love you." I didn't fully appreciate the pattern we had set until the teenage years, which were often fraught with stress, short tempers, and disagreements. After such episodes, the boys' desire to quickly resolve the situation and repair the relationship seemed just as strong as ours.

It's been said that children spell love, T-I-M-E. It's a precious commodity, I know, but making time for them can cure various ills, including meltdowns and power struggles. What better way is there to fill a child's heart with affirmation than sitting down and playing with them? I'll never forget a misunderstanding I had with Zach when he was about 3-or 4-years old. I would occasionally tell him to hurry up and do something and punctuate the command with, "Stop playing." Or "I'm not playing with you," to convey that I was serious. On two occasions he burst into pitiful tears. I asked why he was crying. The first time he wailed, "But playing is my *favorite* thing to dooooo!!" The second time he said, "Because you're not going to play with me anymore." He sounded like he had lost his best friend. Maybe he thought he had. Thank goodness this only happened twice before I got the message -- playing was LOVE to him.

Teaching the boys how to care for themselves, their home, and belongings was another loving way to spend time with them. Children gain valuable skills they will surely need and more importantly, they develop confidence and self-esteem because they can take care of themselves. They can, in turn, use these skills to help other people. That you would take the time to show them the right path is heartening for them, even if they can't put their finger on why they feel good in that moment. They feel empowered, eager even, to apply their new skills in a new situation. Who doesn't like to feel prepared for the situations they face? Everybody wants to help, to know they matter, and that they're valuable in the situations that arise. Knowledge is power. On the flip side, when children don't feel empowered and they don't feel they matter to those around them, they will try to find their own ways to prove they matter and this might result in frustration, dysfunction, and even harm to others.

This brings me to another aspect of the loving power of teaching our children – discipline. Parents often cite this as the most challenging area of parenting. It's no fun, they say. It takes work for sure, but it's worth it.

Mother's Work

Let's think about what discipline is. As defined by Merriam-Webster, discipline can be defined as "training that corrects, molds, or perfects the mental faculties, or moral character" and "orderly or prescribed conduct or pattern of behavior." When identifying the essential elements of raising black children, the authors of *Stickin' To, Watchin' Over, and Gettin' With* cite affection, protection, and correction.[9] I honestly believe this applies to all children, though I understand their angle. Discipline is training, with correction as needed, so our children know how to present and conduct themselves in real-world situations, whether affecting only themselves or others. Discipline is an exercise of teaching and should come from a place of love vs. entitled authority. That teaching varies from family to family, as it is shaded by our values, beliefs, and aspirations, but it all leads to preparation. We all like to feel equipped with the knowledge, skills, and courage for what we are about to experience as we go through life. When you dig deep to the root cause of misbehavior, ranging from poor manners and unkindness all the way to gross mistreatment of others and crimes, you'll find that someone wasn't prepared for the situation they were in and opted to do the easiest thing to avoid

---

[9] Howard C. Stevenson, Gwendolyn Davis, and Saburah Abdul-Kabir; Stickin' To, Watchin' Over, and Gettin' With: An African American Parent's Guide to Discipline, pg. 4, Jossey-Bass of John Wiley & Sons, Inc., CA 2001

facing the insecurity a lack of preparation causes. The external discipline we provide for our children when they are still with us helps engender the internal self-discipline that should serve as their compass for the rest of the journey. We can't let them leave home without it. Self-discipline doesn't guarantee that they won't make mistakes, but that foundation can compress the amount of time it takes for them to face their mistakes, accept the consequences, and course-correct. The younger you start the better, but as I like to tell parents – it's never too late to be the parent you want to be.

Philautia

Essentially, philautia, *is self-love, which can be healthy or unhealthy. Unhealthy self-love is akin to* hubris. *In Ancient Greece, people could be accused of* hubris *if they placed themselves above the gods, or, like certain modern politicians, above the greater good. Many believed that hubris led to destruction, or* nemesis.

Healthy self-love, on the other hand, is akin to self-esteem, which is our cognitive and, above all, emotional appraisal of our own worth. More than that, it is the matrix through which we think, feel, and act, and reflects on our relation to ourselves, to others, and to the world.[10]

Perhaps the greatest offshoot of the love between parents and children is the spark it can give for the child to learn he is lovable and, just as important, capable of loving. I believe awakening such a capacity to love helps them to become invested in life itself. In his book, *The Secure Child*, noted child psychiatrist Stanley Greenspan discussed the importance of warm relationships in helping shape a child's sense of security. In Chapter 3, entitled "Security in Infancy and Early Childhood," Dr. Greenspan said:

"When a baby forms warm, nurturing relationships, he can use them not only in times of stress, challenge, or conflict, but also to maintain an ongoing sense of security. This is possible because children internalize these relationships. Their sense of being a good person, of feeling important, of being worthwhile and worth being cared for all comes from this experience."[11]

---

[10] Burton, Neel, "These Are the 7 Types of Love", Hide and Seek, Psychology Today. 06/25/2016, accessed 07/05/2020, https://www.psychologytoday.com/us/blog/hide-and-seek/201606/these-are-the-7-types-love.

[11] Stanley I. Greenspan; The Secure Child: Helping Our Children Feel Safe and Confident in a Changing World; pg.

Over the years, I have marveled at the evolution of our sons' relationship with each other. They can be competitive, as siblings often are, but they are fierce defenders of each other as well. First and foremost, they share a loving brotherly bond that I believe was formed in the womb. According to research cited in *Scientific American*, unborn twins become aware of each other at 14 weeks gestation.[12] This study was conducted with identical twins, who share a placenta and amniotic sac and can even touch other. Matt and Zach, as fraternal twins, each had his own placenta and amniotic sac, but they seemed to sense each other's movements in the womb. As we got closer to their due date, I imagine things started getting a little tight in there, so whenever one brother started taking a little more than his share of space, the other would give him a little nudge. I was thoroughly entertained!!

We are blessed to live in the same metropolitan area as a good number of our close relatives, which has allowed the boys to build strong relationships with

---

47 – 48; Perseus Publishing of Perseus Books Group; Cambridge, MA 2002

[12] Weaver, Janelle, "Social before Birth: Twins First Interact with Each Other as Fetuses." Scientific American Mind: The Sciences. Scientific American. 01/1/2011, accessed 08/01/2020, https://www.scientificamerican.com/article/social-before-birth/

extended family. Most notable among these relationships were those with both sets of grandparents. Living in such proximity allowed them to participate in everyday aspects of the boys' lives, in addition to holidays and other special occasions. It always warmed my heart to hear the boys' voices go up an octave when they talked with their grandparents, especially on the phone. This time with their grandparents and other extended family provided a vital connection to our family story. The boys' hearts and minds were fed with accounts of their ancestors' history, filled with trials, triumphs, and tall tales. All of these were essential to developing a healthy sense of regard for themselves and the culture that birthed them.

Nowadays, many parents are raising their children far away from extended family. That was the situation with most of the friends in our circle. They made the holidays and special occasions count, either hosting or traveling regularly to visit relatives. They also created fun rituals, like letter writing, making videos and exchanging journals to engage with each other. Sometimes, their children traveled for extended visits during school breaks, allowing them to create special memories with family members they didn't get to see very often.

In some cases, the distance from family members may be more than just physical, such as in the case of conflict, divorce/separation, or other factors. I have seen parents create a loving village for their children among friends, colleagues, or others in the community with whom they share common values and ideals. Church members, coaches, and others can play a powerful role as mentors and guides to help children shape a healthy self-image and sense of pride.

Philia

The hallmark of "philia," or friendship, is shared goodwill. Aristotle believed that a person can bear goodwill to another for one of three reasons: that he is useful; that he is pleasant; and above all, that he is good, that is, rational and virtuous. Friendships founded on goodness are associated not only with mutual benefit but also with companionship, dependability, and trust.[13]

Within our families, we find the genesis of friendship. We're bound by kinship and love, but I submit it is friendship, or friendliness, that allows us to operate in peace and good faith day-to-day. Often when I was out with the boys, people would ask a lot of questions and declare that the boys must be built-in best friends.

---

[13] Burton, Neel, "These Are the 7 Types of Love", Hide and Seek, Psychology Today. 06/25/2016, accessed 07/05/2020, https://www.psychologytoday.com/us/blog/hide-and-seek/201606/these-are-the-7-types-love.

Mother's Work

They do have a special connection, but they had to grow to understand each other and develop a genuine regard for each other over time, just like friends with no blood relation do. I never tried to dictate how they felt about each other as I had seen that play out with other families in dysfunctional ways, breeding pretentiousness, jealousy, and resentment. Feeling is an inside job. Instead, I insisted they treat each other with fairness, courtesy and kindness while allowing the relationship to develop organically.

Our children can also learn lessons about friendships from what we do and what we say. My husband, in particular, has talked to our sons since they were young about the importance of having a few good friends in their lives. They have watched us nurture our friendships. They have seen the support we have extended, and received from, our friends during the good times as well as the tough moments. The boys have also formed their own connections with several of our good friends. It's also been interesting to see them form solid friendships with their peers. When Matt was in elementary school, he and his good friend were on the track team. At track meets, if Matt looked over his shoulder and saw he was ahead in the race, he would slow down to wait for his friend. The coach would yell, "Keep going! You'll see him at the finish line!" I am grateful that the boys each have friends who look out for them also. On the topic of forming social groups, Hill Harper said, "You can't build anything with a flimsy foundation. Friendship is the foundation." As our children venture out from our homes into their schools and into their communities, understanding how to be a friend is indeed an asset.

My mother was a great model for me on how to be a friend. In particular, I learned early on how important girlfriends are. I watched my mother engage and enjoy her friends and witnessed how she supported and was supported by her friends. A few of her friendships have truly been 'til death do us part. My godmother is her oldest friend, and they are still going strong in their eighties and nineties. My godmother was present for anything I've ever done that matters (and probably for a few things that didn't). It didn't occur to me how impactful watching and experiencing my mother's friendships would be until much later.

> *"A friend is one that knows you as you are, understands where you have been, accepts what you have become, and still, gently allows you to grow."*
> *- William Shakespeare*

As I acknowledged earlier, I am blessed with a wide circle of friends whom I cherish greatly. One of my oldest friends joked once that I "collect" them. I don't know that I consciously do that, but I am always open, and I try to preserve the connections I do make in some capacity. Very much like my mother before me, I have one or two friends I can tell anything, including if I robbed a bank. They might laugh with me initially, then surely escort (or even drag) me back to return the stolen cash. I have a few friends with whom I can share certain areas of my life. Then I have friends I enjoy tremendously in the moment, though we don't do a deep dive on our innermost thoughts. For the most part, I take the lead from them. I'm willing to accept what they're comfortable with. I doubt that I am very different from many of you reading this book.

Prior to becoming a mother, I had not consciously considered the notion of seasons of friendship. I was truly a "BFF" kind of gal, with an emphasis on FOREVER. Even if there were long breaks between notes or phone calls, you were my friend until you decided you weren't. Over time, I learned that friendships can change when you make other lifetime commitments like marriage and motherhood. You probably need your cherished friendships more than ever as you adjust to these new responsibilities, but they are harder to feed and nurture than before. Frankly, some of them won't survive that season of your life. I know this all too well. Here's an example of a friend breakup from my own experience:

A friend I'd known for a little over 30 years reached out to tell me, essentially, that I hadn't been such a great friend for at least the last 10 of those years. Our friendship had reached the end of the road and had no place in the bright future she saw for herself. I was taken aback by this, but not entirely shocked as I had witnessed her ending even longer-standing relationships in a similar fashion as she worked to situate her life the way she wanted it. I expressed as much when I initially responded to her text (yes, a text). I just figured it was bound to be my turn one day. And here we were. Her message wasn't long but cited a few grievances. I didn't feel the need to refute them, line by line, or counter with any of my own. I did express my disapproval of her friendship "housecleaning" approach as I had in the past, and also indicated that I felt I certainly had been a good friend to her. My response was brief but sharply worded.

My answer was the wrong one, though. Not only did I know this within three to four hours, I also knew what I should have said instead. More about that in a moment. Fast forward to the next day when I read an article written by a talented blogger friend. The title was "The Accused Cannot Be The Judge"[14]. The article reflected on her experience as a diversity and inclusion trainer. She talked about how people from different cultures, backgrounds, and life experiences come together in the workplace and unwittingly offend each other, with unpleasant

---

[14] Bryant, Randi, "The Accused Cannot Be The Judge," January 4, 2018, accessed, January 8, 2018, https://www.linkedin.com/pulse/accused-cannot-judge-randi-bryant-agenbroad

consequences at best and jarring instances of ageism, sexism, racism, and other –isms, at worst. She pointed out how the accused would often claim they didn't understand the problem, they didn't mean any harm by their behavior, or ultimately, it was the other person's problem for being so thin-skinned. The point of the article was that it didn't matter what the accused thought the other person's feelings about, and reactions to, the event should be. What mattered was how the other person actually experienced it and how he actually felt about it.

This perspective confirmed what I kind of knew when I responded to my friend the first time around. I was on the right track when I didn't try to refute or discredit her specific claims. I was almost home when I resisted the urge to enumerate the ways I felt I had acted as a totally awesome friend. As often happens when you don't leave well enough alone, things went south when I took issue with her process and proceeded to assert, "I HAVE been a good friend to you!" She conveyed to me how she experienced being my friend and her feelings were what mattered. I didn't get to tell her she couldn't have them, whether I agreed or not. A few hours after my response, I knew I should have done better and the blog post confirmed it. The better me wished I had simply said, "I am sorry I failed you. Best of everything to you and your family." Ultimately, that is what I did say and I moved on. I

> *know I'm not perfect at anything, including friendship. I also know I was about as authentically "me" as I could be in that friendship and I don't know how to be anything else.*

This episode with my former friend made me realize that from time to time, many of us avoid holding ourselves accountable when we hurt others, including our children. We don't intend to hurt anyone, but we may frequently discount the feelings of friends, colleagues AND family. How often do we tell our children they shouldn't cry, shouldn't feel angry/mad/sad about something we've done or said? Perhaps, we've told our spouse or partner that she should stop being so sensitive. In fact, we often take great pains to try and talk others out of their feelings: "You're not mad at your brother." "Of course, you want to share with your sister." "That's not a big deal!" After a while, children don't know their own minds or their own hearts. How will they be able to master life without this critical self-knowledge? How can they feel validated in the world if not even in their own home? Don't try to talk your children out of their feelings. Without life experience and context, their feelings are all they have to guide them. Teach them to trust their inner compass. Maybe in the end, my friend was tapping into some inner wisdom when she decided to terminate our relationship. I have to respect that.

Mother's Work

While you may not experience such a dramatic "friend shift," to borrow a phrase from author Jan Yager, be prepared for some movement in your circle. Even as some friendships fade, others may actually deepen during your active parenting years. You might be pleasantly surprised. I am so thankful that throughout everything, I have been able to hold on to my two oldest friends, Michelle and Angelia, from the playpen and first grade through Girl Scouts, summer camp, practical jokes, half-baked schemes, boys, high school, college, young adulting, marriages, celebrating, and mourning. Remember that your friends have seasons in their lives, too. When I was knee-deep in diapers, Michelle was building her career as an educator and earning her Ph.D., while Angelia was married and building a stellar career planning large-scale events. We didn't talk every day, but they carved out time to be simply marvelous godmothers to my sons. The seasons of those relationships that are meant to stick will peacefully align with yours and you'll be able to pick up where you left off. Trust this.

For all the talk about transformation and turning points in pre-existing friendships, I must share that you can look forward to making a few "mom friends" when you have children. Yes, just when you thought you had enough sister-friends, your circle expands. These might be the moms of your children's friends or other ladies you meet while you're out mommin,' or at the grocery store, gym, or hair salon.

Mother's Work

The funny thing is you don't have to know these mom friends very long before the mischief, mayhem, and memories begin. I experienced such a sisterhood a few years back when I injured my ankle just as I started playing basketball in the women's rec league. It turns out all of us were mothers. As I lay on the court in pain, wondering how much damage I had done, how I'd get home, how my sons would get to school the next day, why this had to happen when my husband was out of town, these women figured it ALL out. Well, except the part about my husband being away on business. I'll never forget it. *Beth 1* called for ice. Sandra declared, "Carol has to get to the hospital." *Beth 2* decided she would be the one to drive me to the hospital. Helen volunteered to drive my SUV to my house and talk to my sons. Scratch that. She'd just slip the keys in the mailbox. No need to upset them. Amazingly, with their quick actions and a LARGE dose of divine intervention, I was back home in my own bed a little more than two hours after I hit the floor. When a sisterhood of mothers starts attacking a problem, in short order, you can consider it *handled*. Over the years, I enjoyed special moments with my mom friends, heading off to such attractions as amusement parks, beach excursions, outlet malls, corn mazes, movies, or just coffee talk. Don't discount the value of these friendships.

As we move on, I want to leave you with my take on a few points about friendship among women that resonated with me. Author Sophia Nelson wrote a piece a few years ago entitled "Time to Put the Sister Back in Sisterhood." She starts by saying, "Not every woman will be your best friend, nor should she be invited to be in your inner circle, but *every* woman is deserving of your respect and support when you are able to provide it... Being your sister's keeper should be a reflex."[15] Ms. Nelson suggested we take a mental pledge to do the following for our sisters:

1. <u>Be kind.</u> Just as bad deeds may haunt us later, when you do right by others, kindness has a way of coming back, too.
2. <u>Be patient.</u> We all need encouragement, grace, and support. As my beloved stepfather liked to say, "Carol, they're doing the best they can."
3. <u>Communicate.</u> Don't rely on technology to get an important message to your sister friend. And deliver it personally, not through other people. Do the work to resolve conflicts in a personal and compassionate way.
4. <u>Be empathetic.</u> Seek to understand. Seek to forgive. Assume the best of your sister friend and her intentions.
5. <u>Operate by a code of conduct.</u> Stand for something and walk your talk. When your

---

[15] Nelson, Sophia, "Time to Put the Sister Back in Sisterhood," 02/10/2014, HuffPost, accessed 02/14/2014, https://www.huffpost.com/entry/what-is-sisterhood-really_b_4410051

sisters think of grace, compassion, fairness, and integrity, they should think of you.

Agape

Agape love is unconcerned with the self and concerned with the greatest good of another. Agape isn't born just out of emotions, feelings, familiarity, or attraction, but from the will and as a choice. Agape requires faithfulness, commitment, and sacrifice without expecting anything in return.[16]

Agape is usually cited as the highest form of love; love without limits. In fact, agape is very often used to describe a universal charity and regard shown to all mankind. Although agape is not restricted to love within a family, I want to start there. This foundational love is likely the first form of love our children encounter without even knowing how deep it goes. Their first glimpse of it is likely the affection we lavish upon them through physical touch and our tender words. When our children come into the world, that seed of this love has already been planted in our hearts. We then act on it, willingly and determinedly. There is nothing within our power that we won't do

---

[16] Roat, Alyssa, "What Does Agape Really Mean in the Bible?," Christianity.com. 12/20/2019, accessed 07/09/2020, https://www.christianity.com/wiki/christian-terms/what-does-agape-love-really-mean-in-the-bible

Mother's Work

for them to help them grow, keep them safe, make them happy. We can't imagine anything they could do to make us lose this love supreme that fills us to bursting. From the moment the boys were born and for many years after, folks would ask, "When are you going to have the next one?" or "Don't you want to try for a girl?" I always answered that if God sent me another one, I'd be happy to receive him or her, but I wasn't planning on it. Truth is I had always envisioned having three children, but once my two little guys were born, I fell in love and honestly couldn't imagine being able to spread my love to more children. I know that makes no sense, given that plenty of parents manage to do this every day, but that was my thought at the time. I trust that things have turned out the way they were supposed to, and I have the family God intended for me. I will say agape love for my children has helped me to overcome obstacles I would have gladly retreated from otherwise.

This love within the family can serve to help children develop agape love for those they encounter in school, the community, and in the world. Closely related to teaching them how to do things, as discussed earlier, is helping them see how they can be of service or help to others. It's a way of making them conscious of the fact that their actions have an impact on others for good or not so good.

Mother's Work

Throughout my life, I have experienced wonderful examples of agape being practiced, professionally and socially, in the community. I have a friend who started out as my professional organizer in my home when my children were young. When my friend answers the phone, she announces her name and her company and then says cheerily, "how can I help?" I don't know why, but it sounds far more refreshing and sincere than the tired old, "Can I help you?" we get when we're in the drive-thru lane or some other customer service setting today. You see, she's not asking IF she can help you; she's sure she can, in some form or another. She just needs you to tell her how.

This reminds me of something my Bible Study leader said one day. She said that the Bible is the story of God's creation and, while He doesn't need us to do His great work, we are very much part of His creation as recounted from Genesis to Revelation. Finally, she said, with all the occupations we each perform, we are preserving His creation. For some reason, that was an "Aha" moment for me because I'm not sure I ever thought about any of my jobs that way. In most cases, I pursued them because of particular skills I had combined with the interests I had, and the possibility of being adequately compensated. I didn't necessarily think of my day job as "God's work." I only classified what I did in church or the community that way. I read where President Jimmy Carter once said, "I have one life and one chance to make it count for something… My faith demands that I do whatever I can, **wherever**

I am, **whenever** I can, for **as long as** I can with **whatever** I have to try to make a difference." He has always been committed to service, but that statement is especially poignant given the particularly **"help-full"** life he's led since his presidency ended. He exhibits strong courage and peace now, even as he has battled cancer over the years.

There's always a way to help. James Durst said, "Help one another; there's no time like the present and no present like the time." The seeds of love and friendship along with the talents we help our children cultivate, will give them the raw materials they need. Let's also teach them to collaborate, cooperate, and agitate to get the job done as if God's creation depends on it... because it does.

Gems From My Journey

- Everything children need to know about love, they learn at home.
- Children spell love T-I-M-E.
- Discipline should begin with love.
- Friendship begins at home.
- True friendship is an act of love.

Chapter 6

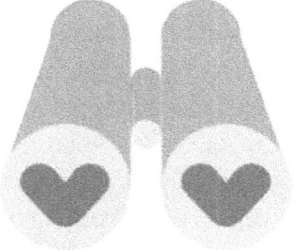

Presence

Remember that saying about the years being short and the days long when you're raising children? That was no joke -- I can't believe how quickly 20 years have gone by. I must admit that in the beginning, I had a hard time settling down to be present with my children. I had this fear of being overwhelmed with taking care of them, and I was always trying to stay two steps ahead of the game. Sometimes it would have been better to just sit and look into their eyes for a few minutes.

Mother's Work

In due time, I came to learn that being organized and in control all the time with one child, let alone two, was pretty unrealistic. Still, I had to create some illusion of order if I was going to be anything close to present for these two little boys. Aside from the boys' sleep schedule, I had to create a routine for getting things done, so my mind wouldn't always be wandering off to what I should be doing instead. Around this time, I read an amazing book called *Time Management from the Inside Out* by Julie Morgenstern. I liked how her approach allowed me to master my time and create a system focused on my values, hopes, and dreams vs. having me design my life to fit some external model or planner. Using suggestions from her book, I created a routine that worked for us. Another catalyst for my transformation was my son's speech therapist. She always had homework for ME after each of his sessions. The assignments required me to make visual tools to reinforce what he was learning with her. That process unleashed creativity such that I also developed games and books to teach him as well as his brother other useful life skills. If I didn't see what I wanted in a store or online, I just made it. One of those creations was the wall calendar I talked about at the beginning of this book. Getting a handle on our busy schedule helped me lighten up and just *be* with my children.

Some of my fondest present moments with my sons happened in my Toyota Sequoia, a.k.a. my apartment. I transported them everywhere in it during the day. I ate in it. I napped in it while I waited for them to finish gymnastics, t-ball, tae kwon do or whatever they were doing. Of course, we took road trips in it, listening to books on tape. Almost anything was fair game, except videos. I was adamant about that. It felt too much like watching TV in the car and I had to draw the line there.

Some folks teased me about being a snob when I banned videos from the car. The fact is, what I treasured most about our car rides were the conversations with the boys, especially their observations, even if they took a long, meandering road to get to a point. I remember attending a parent talk by Rosalind Wiseman, author of *Queen Bees and WannaBes*. She impresses upon us the importance of listening to our children with a statement to the effect that we "should expect to be changed by what we hear." So often we think we know what our children have to say before they say it and we half-listen. Sure, they might say something funny, maybe interesting and, once in a while, informative, but to be *changed* by what you hear them say is profound. I started listening differently after hearing Ms. Wiseman's talk.

Between the two of us, my husband and I made it to all of the boys' school and sporting events. The time spent on those drives to and from was priceless. I recall hearing actor Ben Affleck talking about such moments with his children on similar jaunts, and he

Mother's Work

referred to it as what "happens in the cracks" -- vs. in more carefully choreographed occasions. He was speaking of the unexpected laughter, conversations, and revelations that just naturally sprang up. These treasures are sometimes obscured or even stifled during structured moments or those with external distractions like videos or electronic devices.

Putting forth the effort to be more attuned to my children also made me more inclined to slow down and take in more of what was going on in other situations as well. This was a gift, especially as social media came on the scene. Even we parents get a little carried away and find ourselves at a loss when we go off the grid. You think I'm kidding? Let me ask you something. Do you know why flamingos are pink? I acquired the answer during a visit to the ophthalmologist's office one day. Backstory: I had assumed (and hoped) the visit wouldn't require eye dilation, and I came prepared with a book and my smart phone. No such luck. There I sat in the waiting room with blurred vision, unable to read a thing. My life – interrupted!

I was not alone, as I sat with the other patients who were also unable to scroll or text. When was the last time you went anywhere without seeing folks hypnotized by the small screen, happily ensconced in their own worlds or engaged electronically in THE most important conversation EVER? The grocery

Mother's Work

store? Yeah, right! A red light? Please! The bathroom or church? Forget about it! No place is sacred, or so I thought until I sat at the eye doctor's!

With little else to do in the waiting area, this multi-generational, multi-racial crew struck up a conversation easily, *first* lamenting our current predicament of not being able to read or use our phones. We quickly moved on to how technology has changed the rules of social engagement, how parents and grandparents try to stay connected with today's youth, even how education has changed. Once upon a time, folks had to rely on their family's World Book Encyclopedia or slightly outdated books and microfilm at the library when writing research papers. Now, with Google and Wikipedia, all the latest information you need at your immediate disposal. One of the mothers in the room commented on an advantage of instant data. "At least now we can quickly get answers to silly questions like 'why are flamingos pink?'"

The rest of us laughed and agreed that parenting in this digital age can get tricky. Phones beeping and vibrating at the dinner table, time spent texting instead of connecting in the family room like the good ol' days… and what kind of pigeon language is this texting anyway? LOL! Another mom thought it stood for "lots of love." We enjoyed a few unplugged

Mother's Work

moments, engaged in lively conversation, before we peeled away to complete our respective eye exams.

The good news, of course, is that time away from devices does *not* mean life is interrupted. There are still many opportunities to connect, as my story about the doctor's office demonstrates. Why, I wouldn't even have been in that doctor's office at all if not for a chance conversation with another mom at a presentation on glaucoma. I mentioned that my father had had glaucoma, and at least two of his siblings were also stricken with it. I thought I was on top of it with annual visits to an optometrist. "Oh no," the other mom said. "You have to see an ophthalmologist because they run specific tests to check for glaucoma." Because of that discussion, ophthalmologist visits have become a part of my routine, and I am happy to say the coast is clear for me, so far. Now, why do flamingos, which are born white, turn pink? Oh, I'll tell ya, *BUT* you have to connect with me first.

I think it's also good to be engaged and present with other children and families in your neighborhood. Compared to when I was growing up, some neighborhoods don't have that community feel. People "mind their own business" and "don't want to get involved." I can't believe I'm saying this, but we need to mind each other's business (i.e., look out for each other). We need to embrace even the nosy neighbors – like Steve Urkel from Family Matters, Newman from Seinfeld, or Babette from Gilmore Girls. I know I'm reaching way back, but the truth is they don't make 'em like that anymore. Hey, I might even be one of these characters. One day, as I came down the driveway walking my dog, I hear this: "Oh, I see it. I'm going down to get it." The sight I'm seeing? Three children looking down a manhole connected to a sewer located right at the corner of my yard. Without even thinking, my mouth opens and out comes, "Oh, no you are not!" They looked at me in shock for about two seconds. They'd only lived on our block a little while and they knew my children from school, but I hadn't gotten to know them well yet. After a few moments, the only girl piped up and respectfully said, "Yes, I am. My dad's gonna help us." Right about then, Dad, whom I had spoken to often, comes walking out, in his socks. One of the boys said, "Dad, why are you wearing socks? You can't go in the manhole in socks. You need shoes." Dad said with a smirk, "Because I have no intention of going down into the sewer." He promptly lifted the very heavy manhole cover (NEVER underestimate the strength of kids on a half-baked mission) and placed it in its proper position. I said to myself, "Mission Accomplished." But I think I caught a side eye from one of the kids as if she was saying, "If she hadn't slowed us down…" Seriously though, I'm glad I was there to protect them. How many times have we seen folks stand by while their fellow man is being harmed, possibly even capturing it on video and posting the

Mother's Work

episode on some social media page? While none of my childhood escapades was taped, many were foiled by, you got it, nosy folks in my neighborhood. Thank God for them. They just wanted me to stay on track and to have a future. We have to pass this idea of neighborliness, and being present for others, on to our children. They're becoming numb to the shocking things they're seeing and hearing. We can share the words of Jesus to his disciples, "Truly I tell you, whatever you did for one of the least of these brothers and sisters of mine, you did for me." We must tell our children not to worry if they aren't sure what they have to offer or where to start. As Elbert Hubbard said, "Your neighbor is the man who needs you. "

As I finish this book, most of our country is under quarantine, due to the outbreak of the Coronavirus (COVID-19). This time in the house has made me more appreciative of those experiences I had outside of it. I am even more committed to taking a deep breath and settling in to being where I am. Eckhart Tolle said, "Most people treat the present moment as if it were an obstacle that they need to overcome." He goes on to say, "Since the present moment is life itself, it is an insane way to live." I can agree with that, can't you? We miss so much by merely going through the motions. What have I noticed since I started paying attention? I perform much better when I cut out sugar. I'm hearing from my sons more often. When I am truly present at the meetings or in classes I teach, I occasionally say something interesting and most definitely hear something intriguing. And as Mordecai said to his cousin Esther as he urged her to intercede with the king on behalf of their Jewish brethren, "And who knows but that you have come to your position for such a time as this?" If you are not mindful of the moment, a word may not be said, an action may not be taken; even a look might not be exchanged at a time when that is just what was needed, and YOU were the one to do it. Don't underestimate the impact of your presence – it is a gift -- to yourself and to others.

Gems From My Journey

- Set yourself up to be present. Get organized – in your physical space and your mental space.
- Set a routine for your family. Get plenty of rest.
- Be where you are. Take it in, fully.
- Make a difference with your presence.

Mother's Work

Chapter 7

Peace

And the peace of God which surpasses all understanding, will guard your hearts and your minds in Christ Jesus.– Philippians 4:7

Most anybody who knows me well would certainly understand motherhood would take up an enormous amount of space with me. To make it manageable, I had to focus on what was absolutely necessary and let the rest fall away. I am still learning about TV shows and music that I totally missed in the early 2000s because I just didn't have the bandwidth to take that in when the boys were little. I knew I had to honor my journey and be at peaceful assurance that God would make me aware of what I needed to know and would provide what I needed.

Once I was asked to name my favorite memory as a mother. When I thought about it, I realized that it wasn't a single event, but one that repeated itself EVERY day – bedtime. It was such a special time of closeness with zero-stress, starting when my boys were young. Aside from stuffed animals, there were no distractions like TV or noisy games in their bedroom. We set the mood, softly playing CDs from the likes of Josh Groban, Norah Jones, and India Arie. The boys would wind down in their baths and they looked forward to curling up to read with us. We read a devotional message first, and then one book that each of the boys selected. We continued this routine well after they could read for themselves and on vacations. If there was one word to describe these moments, it would be P E A C E F U L. Oh, how I looked forward to peace at the end of every day. At least that's what peace looked like for me. Some parents find peace in chaos and cacophony and that's OK. As long as you can find it, that's what matters.

When I work with parents, they often come with frustrations about kids fighting, talking back, not cooperating. They also talk about things they miss doing like book club, girls/guys night out. I think they are also searching for peace. We love our children and in those season when they depend on us most, it can be hard to reclaim those moments for ourselves. But we must, just not all at once. I first began to reclaim my peace by polishing my nails. Sounds like a simple thing, but I used my hands to give constantly and washed them about twenty times every day. I wanted to treat them right, the way I used to before I had children. I'd make a big production of it – laying out all my tools in the bathroom, putting on my favorite music and spending time with myself. This mini retreat rejuvenated me and trust me, my family benefited also. Little by little, I started finding and sometimes rediscovering other ways to usher peace into my life.

Bible study brings me a great deal of peace. When the boys were little, I studied alone aside from the time I read with them. After they got older, I joined a women's Bible study that I truly look forward to each week. Attending Sunday worship also brings me peace. Since the days right after I graduated from college, I just feel my weeks go better if I attend church on Sunday. Back then, I was so protective of this time on Sunday mornings that I didn't take any phone calls or interact with people until after church. My girlfriends thought this was a bit much. I've loosened up since then, but yes, I'm serious about peace.

Mother's Work

Along with external rituals and practices, I realized I had some vital, internal work to do. First, I had to let go of the idea that I am going to get this thing called mothering right, as in perfectly right. I had to became comfortable with the fact that I am going to make some bad calls. When I needed to retract statements or rescind actions I took with my children, I mustered up the courage and humility to do just that. It was important that they knew, without a doubt, they were worthy of the respect and consideration of an apology when it was due from me or anybody else. I decided that as long as I was doing the best I could with what I knew at the time, I could be at peace - as a parent or in any role I was trying to fill.

Another area where I struggled to find peace was accepting my sons' decisions as they got older. For years, we'd been teaching them to recognize the consequences of their choices where behavior was concerned. As teens, they were making bigger decisions that could have implications for the future. I remember when Zach decided to give up basketball in high school. He had come to love the game in middle school and invested many hours and our dollars training. He played his first two years of high school, but as he managed his rigorous course load with the relentless practice schedule, he realized that his life was out of balance. I enjoyed watching him play and as I mentioned earlier, my experience supporting him had inspired me to take the game up myself. All this prompted my initial reaction: "Now, let's not be hasty." He was resolute about his decision and a wonderful thing happened – he had time to explore other school activities and tackle his studies at a whole new level. He even found time to play basketball on his own terms, first with weekly pickup games and later with his friends on a team in the local rec league. The team went undefeated and won the championship! I ultimately accepted the fact that he made the decision that was right for him.

Sometimes, we are indeed constrained by our knowledge or access to information. Other times, we might just be constrained by time – it's not our season to do something different. We have to make peace with that. I have thought a lot about this over the past few years. There has been so much change in our family and in my life, specifically. Our sons went off to college, leaving us with the proverbial empty nest. I miss them terribly when they are away, but I am reclaiming some of what I have missed of my own life during the years that I focused on raising them. I wouldn't trade those years, but it is good to rediscover some of the interests and aspirations I shelved to be more fully engaged in their upbringing. Thankfully, I planted seeds and made small investments here and there in areas that interested me like parent education, community involvement, and philanthropy and now I am seeing the growth. I have to be honest and say that I sometimes watched wistfully as friends climbed the corporate ranks or built businesses, but I had to find a way to be at peace with God's timing in my life. This is my season! At a time when many of my peers are winding down their careers and renovating their long-empty nests, I am winding up! Coming at this time in my life, this growth and opportunity almost feels like validation of the decision I made to step off the treadmill of my career and do something different after my children were born. The validation does not mean I was the perfect mother. It just says I did the best I could, I met my children's needs, and it's OK now to do more for me.

During this season, I have been able to get out and meet more people. I am elevating the platform of my radio show, and I am finally getting this book written. I am investing in myself again, acquiring critical knowledge, and navigating the next phase of my professional life. I have attracted more opportunities to engage and speak than at any other time in my career. Aside from being named DC Mother of the Year®, I was named Radio Personality of the Year at SpeakerCon, a premier conference for industry leaders and professional speakers. How cool is that?

It's funny when I consider that when my parents were this age, they looked forward to retirement. Today, I see that retirement looks very different now. Due to advancements in healthcare and the dissemination of information on fitness and nutrition, we take better care of ourselves, and the window of middle age is shifting – people are living AND working longer. I see this phenomenon in entertainment, business, politics, and many other arenas. I was inspired by an article about Gayle King, lead anchor for CBS This Morning since 2012. Though she certainly paid her dues, building an impressive journalism career over 20+ years, she's now riding a resurgent wave, after having been out of the TV news game for a while to focus on her role as Editor-At- Large at *O, the Oprah Magazine*. That's unheard of, particularly in the broadcast news industry, where female news anchors have often been pushed aside as early as 47 or 50 years old. She's changing the narrative in that space. I'm changing the narrative in mine. There was a conference for mothers seeking speakers for various workshops. I wondered if I was too old for their demographic but said "what the heck?" and submitted a proposal. I was selected because in their words, they were "seeking expertise, not just people who dabbled in a subject."

I recently saw a quote in my newsfeed that said, "The people who say the glass is half full or half empty have it all wrong; the glass can be refilled!" My cup is running over, and I feel at peace with where I am!

Gems From My Journey

- Make home a place where your children can find peace.
- Practice self-care. Create moments of peace for yourself.
- When you know you have done the best you could with what you have, be at peace with yourself.
- Be at peace knowing you can't control everything. This includes your children's decisions.
- Be at peace with God's plan for you.

A Final Word

"Motherhood: All love begins and ends there."
– Robert Browning

So, what *is* mother's work? It's that special brand of energy, wisdom, finesse, and devotion you bring to the children who have sojourned to be with you. They may have been birthed through your body or placed in your arms through some other divine miracle. Surely, they have taken up residence in your hearts, occupied your mind, and brought an undeniable sparkle to your eyes. You have accepted your charge to nurture in them a confident and courageous spirit to advance toward the purpose and promise life holds for them.

Others will also be appointed to pour out goodness into your child's life, but only you have this divine assignment. It's not father's work, it's not grandmother's work, it's not teacher's work; it's mother's work. You don't do it for show or "the dough." You do it with passion and conviction and without shame. You do it with love. In return, you are rewarded with a special bond that informs your actions -- knowing when to push, pull, nudge, or provide cover. It's that knowing that activates like a drone on a mission through space, time, and distance when your children need you and when your children are in trouble. Your heart is always on call. That's mother's work -- never easy but abundantly fruitful.

There is no one right way to do mother's work, though there may be some wrong ways if you don't start with the needs of *your* children. So, do lean in and learn -- they're fascinating. If you do, it will be a transformative journey for you as well as your children.

It matters that you are in your child's life and the impact of your work will be seen for years to come. When you have done the best, you can with what you have, it will be a thing of beauty and a work you will be proud to sign your name to.

Mother's Work

Appendix A

Real Beauty
(Originally posted on my blog at www.carolmuleta.com.)

"Some women feel the need to act like they're never scared, needy or hurt; like they're as hardened as a man. I think that's dishonest. It's ok to feel delicate sometimes. Real beauty is in the fragility of your petals. A rose that never wilts isn't a rose at all."
- Crystal Woods

As I gaze at this bouquet of flowers, I note that it is far from its finest hour. Yet, I treasure it. It was the centerpiece on our table at a luncheon I attended last week during the 84th Annual Convention of American Mothers, Inc. I had the winning seat at my table and my prize was this lovely pitcher from the immensely popular Pioneer Woman collection. It was filled with beautiful flowers in full bloom. Of course, I had already won in so many ways.

It was my privilege to attend the conference after being named the 2019 Mother of the Year® for the DC

Mother's Work

Metro area by American Mothers, a nonpartisan nonprofit organization which owns the trademark to Mother of the Year® and is the official sponsor of Mother's Day. American Mothers is committed to serving as an advocate on issues affecting our country's 85 million mothers and their children. The organization has been honoring state and national honorees since 1935, with help from Eleanor Roosevelt, who helped elevate the day of observance. American Mothers, Inc. named its first black Mother of the Year® in 1946!

I was part of a special cohort of Mothers chosen to represent their states, with 46 actually attending the convention. I was awed by the energy, courage, candor, and kindness of this group. I had read most of the bios, so I already knew I would be in very special company. However, I was blown away by the speeches on Day 2 of the conference. We were challenged to address America in a speech themed "America, this is your mother speaking..." Moms being moms, you know we could have gone on for hours — alas, we only had three minutes. Accustomed to making magic out of mania, we dynamic mothers rose to the occasion, delivering heartfelt testimonies of triumph and loss, joy, and pain, uncertainty, and revelation. We approached the task through lenses tinted by different races, religions, and regions of the country as well as different educational backgrounds, career experiences, and lifestyles, but we all cheered when the underdog won, were outraged at insensitivity and injustice, mourned the losses, and were in awe of the sacrifices our sisters had made. And we had become sisters, a real "momraderie." There was a sense of knowing among us only mothers possess. A knowing that on most days not all of the flowers in the bouquet will be in bloom at the same time. There will be some curled or wilted petals as trials set upon us and dry, discolored leaves as our resolve is tested. Yet, like flowers pushing through concrete, there are always signs of hope and beauty in our bouquet.

Leading up to that year's convention, American Mothers launched a nationwide study to find *What Matters to Moms* through the American Mothers Project. Preliminary findings indicated these top three concerns: access to mental health services and resources, access to affordable childcare, and quality education for all children. On Day 3, we got a glimpse of how we could use our knowledge and personal experiences to make a difference in our country. First, we witnessed an engaging bipartisan discourse between Rep. Debbie Lesko (R-AZ) and Rep. Brenda Lawrence (D-MI) about such topics as women in leadership, sex trafficking, and foster care. Next, we headed to Capitol Hill to meet with our elected representatives, armed with our states' respective concerns as well as the early data from the American Mothers Project. We felt powerful. We were powerful. As the convention began to wind down, I was thankful that one of my college-age sons was able to join me at the gala on the last day, along with my husband and mother. Without them, and my other son, none of this would have been possible. Together, they have watched me and often caused me to stretch and grow, and to stay firmly planted with arms folded when I might otherwise have given up. After my son listened to the speakers that evening, he wondered aloud why practically all of the discussion centered on the love and nurturing mothers provide. He thought it sounded patriarchal and somewhat dismissive of all that mothers do. He said he appreciated my staying home to raise him and his brother. He also remarked that, "[Love and nurturing] was the least of what you did. You did so much more – you were *working.*" I was touched by his sentiments, but I had to remind him that love and nurturing were at the heart of all the work I did. It's how moms everywhere make everything fall into place like only they can. Motherhood. It's a thing of real beauty.

About the Author

Carol Muleta is a Parenting Strategist and Consultant. She created The Parenting 411™, a portal where she engages parents and awakens the JOY in their journey through workshops, webinars, and private consultations. She teaches them to address challenging behavior, build strong family connections, and foster their children's success in academics and life. Carol has been immersed in parent education nearly 17 years and became certified as a Parent Educator and Consultant along the way. She was named 2019 DC Mother of the Year® by American Mothers, Inc. She co-founded a parent education and consulting company where she designed parenting programs, consulted with families, and co-created Gardener Parent Method™. She hosts the Parenting 411 radio show, where she explores various matters affecting family life from discipline and communications to work-life harmony and co-parenting. Carol was named Radio Personality of the Year at SpeakerCon 2019. She is a contributing author of <u>Courageous Enough To Launch: Stories & Strategies of Everyday Women Who Faced Their Fears to Launch Thriving Businesses</u> and <u>I Am A Victor: Stories of individuals who victoriously turned their pain into purpose</u>. Carol and her husband are the proud parents of two young adult sons.

Mother's Work

About The Parenting 411™

The Parenting 411™ is a portal I created to present contemporary parenting perspectives as well as conventional wisdom, curated through personal experience, my work as a certified parent educator, and interviews with leading thinkers on the topic. I give parents the tools they need to enrich and nurture their children's healthy growth and development while fostering good communication and cultivating warm, respectful family relationships. I engage directly with parents through workshops, webinars, and private consultations. It is my mission to deliver "information parents need from sources they can trust.™"

To learn more, visit:	www.carolmuleta.com
Twitter:	@TheParenting411
Facebook:	The Parenting 411
Instagram:	the_parenting_411
YouTube:	The Parenting 411

www.ingramcontent.com/pod-product-compliance
Lightning Source LLC
Chambersburg PA
CBHW071005160426
43193CB00012B/1921